T0341867

Pagan Portals

Hestia

Goddess of Hearth, Home & Community

What people are saying about

Hestia

Although not as well-known as Her Olympian siblings, Hestia played an essential role in ancient Greek religion. But hearth and home remain the sacred spaces around which communities are built – as such, Hestia's warmth and shelter are just as important and healing in today's fractured world as they were millennia ago. And we are very lucky to have Irisanya Moon to guide us to Her. In the pages of *Pagan Portals -- Hestia*, Moon presents a welcoming and understandable portrait of a primeval deity. Through accessible exercises and meditations, along with insight into her personal relationship with Hestia, Moon provides readers with gentle yet sturdy rituals, modern correspondences, and practical spiritual tools, allowing them to venerate the goddess of the hearth in a way that is comforting, contemporary, and effective.

Thumper Forge, author of *Virgo Witch: Unlock the Magic of Your Sun Sign*

Hestia is the Greek Goddess of the hearth fires, the home, and the community. She is a virgin Goddess in that she chose to remain single. However, she was also at the heart of family life for people in Classical times, being honoured in the fire that burnt at the centre of every home. Unlike most other Greek deities, she is peace-loving and promotes harmony in the community. In this lovely book, Irisanya Moon delves into Hestia's history and mythology, but also shows how she can be venerated by modern Pagans. Irisanya offers a range of practical ways to develop a relationship with Hestia, including visualisation, storytelling, cookery, cleaning the home, serving the community, and engaging in hearth magic. This book is a superb introduction to Hestia's place in the Greek pantheon as well as an insightful guide to working with her today.

Lucya Starza, author of Pagan Portals titles *Candle Magic, Poppets and Magical Dolls, Scrying,* and *Rounding the Wheel of the Year* as well as the novel *Erosion*

In a time when it can feel as if we've lost our sense of community, Irisanya Moon reminds us of the Goddess Hestia. Within these pages, we are guided to know more and find a place with this delightfully elegant and wise Deity. This is a vital offering at a time when it is most needed in the world.

Lisa McSherry, author of *Travel Magic* and *A Witch's Guide to Crafting Your Practice*

An indispensable book for anyone building community, creating home, or seeking the goddess Hestia. Containing historical threads, personal experience, rituals, and practical steps, this book is an introduction to an important goddess and an illumination of the magic of the hearth, in all its forms!

Halo Quin, pagan storyteller, community weaver, and author of books including *Storytelling for Magic* and *Folktales, Faeries, and Spirits*

Pagan Portals
Hestia

Goddess of Hearth, Home & Community

Irisanya Moon

**MOON
BOOKS**

London, UK
Washington, DC, USA

CollectiveInk

First published by Moon Books, 2025
Moon Books is an imprint of Collective Ink Ltd.,
Unit 11, Shepperton House, 89 Shepperton Road, London, N1 3DF
office@collectiveinkbooks.com
www.collectiveinkbooks.com
www.moon-books.net

For distributor details and how to order please visit the 'Ordering' section on our website.

Text copyright: Irisanya Moon 2024

ISBN: 978 1 80341 589 5
978 1 80341 716 5 (ebook)
Library of Congress Control Number: 2023949952

All rights reserved. Except for brief quotations in critical articles or reviews, no part of this book may be reproduced in any manner without prior written permission from the publishers.

The rights of Irisanya Moon as author have been asserted in accordance with the Copyright, Designs and Patents Act 1988.

A CIP catalogue record for this book is available from the British Library.

Design: Lapiz Digital Services

UK: Printed and bound by CPI Group (UK) Ltd, Croydon, CR0 4YY
Printed in North America by CPI GPS partners

We operate a distinctive and ethical publishing philosophy in all areas of our business, from our global network of authors to production and worldwide distribution.

Contents

In a culture that often prioritizes and celebrates rugged individualism and separateness, Hestia welcomes us home. Her magick invites togetherness and shared resources by cultivating spaces of belonging and community. May Hestia call us back to our homes to celebrate families of all shapes, sizes, and forms, creating sustainable structures for ongoing collaboration and nourishment.

Acknowledgments

It makes sense to begin with acknowledging those who have helped me along the way to this book, and many others. The energy of Hestia is not one of singularity and individuality. She walks into spaces of families, groups, and communities.

I want to thank Moon Books, and especially Trevor Greenfield, for continuously supporting my writing through encouragement, constructive criticism, and reminders that I'm still not doing the formatting or references correctly. (One day!)

In addition, I would like to thank my community, in its ever-evolving definition and form. The idea for this book came out of a conversation I had while sitting on the couch of my dear friend, Jarrah, who lives in Australia. I was there to teach at a Witchcamp and I had a few days to rest before the planning began. He and I were talking about community and its troubles, as well as how to bring people together again. I thought of Hestia and how people come together around the hearth, literally and figuratively.

And that also brought me to my beloved mentor and friend, Copper Persephone. She died in 2020 and she was fiercely committed to hearth magick. With my friend and her inspiration, I realized building a relationship with Hestia could offer insights into creating sustainable communities. With the ever-growing challenge of modern society and insidious ways of causing division, I know we need to rely on each other more than ever. Sometimes it feels like no one is coming to save us; and we need to save ourselves.

So I call to Hestia in this book as an ally and friend. I acknowledge that my work is not done alone, even though I might be sitting at a laptop in my home by myself. I am the product of teachers and beloveds. Those dear ones who invited me into their homes and their hearths.

I thank them all. To name everyone would be more than this book's word count.

If you think you might be on the list, you are. Thank you. I appreciate you.

Author's Note

In most of my books, I start off with a few things to remember before you read my writing. I do this to help create context for the way I approach working with deities. And to be honest, I also do this because some reviewers seem to write about my books without taking into consideration my included explanations. Fingers crossed, dear reader, that this note might be found and even read this time.

First, I use the term 'godds' to talk about deities. I use this to ensure a more gender-full and gender-expansive experience. I do not believe that godds can be confined to one gender or any, and certainly not to any of the constrictive words of the English language. While I do use pronouns and I will use She/Her for Hestia, know this is not a final determination of gender. I use pronouns that I have used in my personal workings with the godds; you are in choice about what you use in your time with a godd. I will also capitalize She/Her when talking about Hestia, in honor of being the godd of focus in this book.

Second, I realize that I talk about godds from my perspective, my experience, and through my personal lens. I believe that personal gnosis is a valid approach to deity worship. I also include source material and writings from other perspectives. My goal is to bring together as many viewpoints as I can, without creating a dense and inaccessible text. But this does mean you may not agree with my interpretations, which is great. My intention is not to write a book that is the last note on a godd. I write to offer a foundation from which you might create your own relationship with a godd.

Let's also note that while I will use the phrase 'Ancient Greece,' it is not a monolith. There is no one agreed-upon description of what Ancient Greece was, just as there are multiple ways to pronounce Greek words, depending on where and when they arrived. I offer this to remind readers that you may come across conflicting information, and this is completely understandable when mythology is less of a solid answer and more of an idea in flux.

Finally, the Pagan Portals series of books is meant to offer short, concise, and not complete writings on deities and other topics. These books are not comprehensive, and they will leave some aspects and items out. This is not done with malice, but rather to give readers a budget- and attention span-friendly option to hear what one writer thinks about a godd. It's a starting point for longer study and research if you like.

I am honored to be talking about Hestia, whose influence on me has been subtle and pervasive at the same time. My hope is that this book brings Her into your kitchen or to your microwave, and from there, She might tell you about how to keep the fires burning for the community.

Introduction

I can still remember how steep the ground was from the parking spaces to the yurt. When I close my eyes, I can remember the way the soil and grass would give way during the rainy season, and how I needed to slow down as though I were traversing ice or snow. The light from the small plastic windows would emanate, granting a small beacon of welcoming for those who traveled here for classes and other events.

The yurt was (and still is) a round structure with strong canvas sides, able to withstand the winds and rains of northern California. This structure had been used in another city before moving up to its current placement, so it was accustomed to holding space for community.

The first time I entered the yurt was for my first Reclaiming core class, Elements of Magick. The teachers were Copper Persephone and Diana Melisabee, and they would become my mentors and guides into the Reclaiming community. Both committed to hearth magick, you didn't even need to know this to feel it. From the warmth of the fire in the yurt to the (seemingly) un-ending snacks and meals, this yurt space may have been a classroom, but it also became a home.

I can't remember if Hestia's name was uttered here, as there are many memories of classes, workshops, rituals, trainings, meetings, conflict resolutions, rites of passage, mistakes, arguments, celebrations, and more to consider. I'm sure She was a part of the magick and that She was invoked at some point, and even if not in name, She was called forth in spirit. Many times.

Hestia's energy of hearth magick didn't make sense to me, as I was never called to cooking or tending of food. But the first time I taught in that yurt, I realized why communities need the hearth. The hearth is the place of coming together, no matter what is happening in the outside world. It is a place of safety and congruence. It is a place of belonging, as everyone is welcome, and everyone has a place at the table.

When the hearth is acknowledged and revered, community knows itself better, tends itself better, and weathers the complicated nature of being a human with other humans. I've met Hestia in the actions of service, in the ways I still make sure there is enough hot water and toilet paper during class times, even though I teach in other spaces now.

It is Hestia who reminds me that people who feel welcome are people who feel safe. She is clear that Her magick is not just about food, but about nourishment. She might be the deity to help you with fermenting a vegetable, but She is also a deity who reminds me that holding someone's hand is just as supportive to the group.

Hestia is by my side and holding my shoulders as I lift the heavy glass water pitcher and pull the seating cushions from the tall shelves. She is in my ear as I decide what to bring for a potluck or how I could help that one person feel a little more at home. Hestia continues to influence me in the way that I would rather help people feel welcome than to make sure they know how to perfectly cast a circle.

I know Hestia in the moments when I make mistakes in community and try to repair them immediately, and She is there when I stand by the side of someone who takes accountability for their actions. Her magick is the magick of true belonging, though not without responsibility and collaboration. You are so very welcome to Her table.

Pull up a seat and join the conversation.

Chapter 1

Encountering Hestia

Hestia, in the high dwellings of all, both deathless gods and men who walk on earth, you have gained an everlasting abode and highest honor: glorious is your portion and your right. [5] For without you mortals hold no banquet, —where one does not duly pour sweet wine in offering to Hestia both first and last.

And you, Slayer of Argus, Son of Zeus and Maia, messenger of the blessed gods, bearer of the golden rod, [10] giver of good, be favorable and help us, you and Hestia, the worshipful and dear. [9] Come and dwell in this glorious house in friendship together; [11] for you two, well knowing the noble actions of men, aid on their wisdom and their strength.

Hail, Daughter of Cronos, and you also, Hermes, bearer of the golden rod! Now I will remember you and another song also.

Evelyn-White, Hugh G.,
The Homeric Hymns and Homerica

If you've studied the Greek godds for any time, you will likely notice, because it's hard to miss, the drama of being a godd in this pantheon. There are affairs, fights, and controversies. From Zeus and his many lovers to Aphrodite and her disdain for Psyche, the Greek gods are often in conflict and disarray. To me, that's what makes them so approachable and accessible in my magickal practice.

But then there is Hestia. While She is considered one of the 12 Olympians, She isn't mentioned in *The Odyssey* or *The Iliad*, though She is mentioned in *Theogony*. In fact, it might seem that Hestia is pretty boring, outside of the circumstances of Her birth. I mention this because it is an interesting contrast to how She was celebrated and revered in everyday Greek life.

> The power worshiped in the hearth never fully developed into a person; since the hearth is immovable Hestia is unable to take part even in the procession of the gods, let alone in the other antics of the Olympians (Burkert 170).

Hestia isn't one for drama, or it wasn't captured in writing. In any case, She is a steady, solid figure in the Greek pantheon, and someone who continues to influence family life.

Who is Hestia?
Ἑστια | Hestia | Vesta | Hearth

Often pronounced **HEHS-tee-ah**, Hestia's agreed upon meaning is 'hearth' and Her Roman counterpart is Vesta. She is most commonly defined as the goddess of the hearth and home. While there aren't many stories about Her, the worship of Hestia was essential in the life of Ancient Greece. Hestia was the one to which you would make sacrifices before any other godd.

> Hestia, Histie in Ionian, is the normal word for the hearth, the centre of house and family. To banish or destroy a family is to drive out a hearth. The polis community also has as its centre a communal hearth which stands in a temple or in the Prytaneion[1] (Burkert 170).

Researchers have also noted:

The etymology of the word hestia remains somewhat obscure. Some have traced it to the Proto-Indo-European roots *wes ("burn") and *h₂wes- ("dwell, pass the night, stay") ...According to Robert S. P. Beekes, the etymology of Hestia is most likely pre-Greek.[2]

Hestia is present in the everyday lives at the hearths of every home, as well as at main hearth structures for cities and within government spaces. If the city decided to move to a new place, a flame from the original hearth would be moved as well to start the new hearth's fire. The importance of the fire can also be seen as the energy of authority and community, as this is the place where people come together. With all of this said, there are few temples to Hestia in the time of Ancient Greece.

In the depictions of Hestia, She is dressed modestly and sometimes veiled, often holding a flowered branch and a kettle. While it doesn't appear that Hestia had epithets like other Greek godds did, I did find She could be referred to as 'Beloved' or 'Eternal.' In an article by Thomas Apel and Avi Kapach, they note:

> In some later sources, Hestia did have a handful of epithets, among them basileia ("queen"), chloomorphos ("verdant"), and aidios ("eternal").[3]

There are ongoing debates about whether Hestia is one of the original 12 Olympians, but it was Socrates who observed that in one Greek dialect variant the word ουσια [ousia] is εσσια [essia], or primary, which closely resembles Hestia (Sedley 153).

> Hestia was closely connected with Zeus, god of the family in its external relation of hospitality and its internal unity. She was also associated with Hermes, the two

representing domestic life on the one hand, and business and outdoor life on the other. In later philosophy Hestia became the hearth goddess of the universe.[4]

With this collection of insights into Hestia, it becomes clear that She was an important figure, as Her energy was central to homes and governments. While this seems like a simple assembly of facts, what I notice is how these places where Hestia is revered are places that impact larger groups and societal concerns.

For example, it could be said that without Hestia's influence, the act of sacrificing for the greater or common good might not be so tightly ingrained in that society. And when we move Hestia into modern times, it becomes clear how bringing Her worship and reverence back might be a way to return to a more community-based attitude in the Western world of rugged individualism. It can also be noted that Hestia's influence in society also seems to support the importance of shared family values, with 'family' being a loosely defined group of people.

Demure and understated, Hestia has also been described as less of a human figure and more of an idea. She is the embodiment of coming together to support each other and to support the family or government unit. Hestia is said to be the being to which you offer your devotion so as to receive blessings in return. She is the one who would allow for domestic bliss in a household. If She was not revered, the home would not feel like a home.

A Virgin Goddess

Vesta (Greek Hestia) was the goddess of the hearth, both public and domestic. The hearth with its undying flame symbolized the continuity of both family and community, and extinction of the fire was a grave matter. Tending the

family hearth was the responsibility of the daughter of
the household...Since a virgin belongs to no man, she
can incarnate the collective, the city; she can belong to
everyone (Pomeroy 210).

Within the Greek stories, there are several goddesses who are
noted to be virgins, including Athena, Artemis, and Hestia.
However, it is also true that the idea of virginity may have had
other meanings, depending on the translation and the context.
For example, some scholars have noted Artemis' virginity was
more likely about her sovereignty than about whether she has
sexual relations with anyone. It is more likely that she was one
unto herself, meaning she made her own decisions outside of
being beholden to a man.

There are also writings that speak of the idea of virginity
being a sacrifice that was given to be a priestess, but that the
terms of that agreement might end after a certain period of
time. That is, if you were celibate during your priestess training,
when it ended, you did not have to continue that commitment.

Hestia is called both the eldest and youngest daughter
of Kronos; many gods wooed her, but she swore to
remain forever a virgin. This accords with the sexual
taboos surrounding the hearth; it is the daughters of the
household who tend the hearth fire, a fire which is also
experienced as a phallic force. Thus Hestia sits at the
centre of the household 'receiving fatty offerings'; she
never attained an importance comparable to that of the
Roman Vesta (Burkert 170).

In the story of Hestia, however, it seems clear that She asked
to be celibate and thus remained a virgin. This seems to be
supported also by the idea that Hestia was not embodied in

many of the stories, and since She was less of a human-figure and more of an influence, it's understandable that She would also be one unto Herself.

A fully realized female tends to engender anxiety in the insecure male. Unable to cope with a multiplicity of powers united in one female, men from antiquity to the present have envisioned women in 'either-or' roles (Weigle 76).

And it is also wise to remember that in many of the translations of Greek myths, women are seen as either whores or virgins, which is likely a way to make certain goddesses more palatable to a reader. But in times where translations are questioned more frequently, it is reasonable to question whether the 'simplicity' of a goddess is really that simple. There may be things missing from translations that would show a more multifaceted being.

For added complexity, there are some source tests that might indicate a relationship between Hermes and Hestia.

Hestia, in the high dwellings of all, both deathless gods and men who walk on earth, you have gained an everlasting abode and highest honour: glorious is your portion and your right. For without you mortals hold no banquet, —where one does not duly pour sweet wine in offering to Hestia both first and last.

And you, slayer of Argus, Son of Zeus and Maia [i.e., Hermes], messenger of the blessed gods, bearer of the golden rod, giver of good, be favourable and help us, you and Hestia, the worshipful and dear. Come and dwell in this glorious house in friendship together; for you two, well knowing the noble actions of men, aid on their wisdom and their strength.

Hail, Daughter of Cronos, and you also, Hermes, bearer of the golden rod!
Homeric Hymn to Aphrodite" (XXIX:1-12), Hesiod, The Homeric Hymns, and Homerica, edited & translated by Hugh G. Evelyn-White

Trance Work: Connecting with Hestia

As you continue to deepen into a relationship with Hestia (or any godd), I invite you to consider taking a journey to meet Her. This can act as a simple introduction or a reconnection, depending on your current relationship status.

My style of trance work is from the Reclaiming Witchcraft tradition and is informed by hypnosis practices. This trance will begin with a simple induction to soothe and settle your body, then it will lead you through a journey to find Hestia, give you space to have whatever experience you might have, and then will lead you back into the present moment.

Unlike other guided meditation or journey practices, my style of trance is not designed to tell you what to experience, but rather it offers you a container in which something is likely to happen. I do not want to tell you what your experience might be with a godd, but I do want to help you have the best conditions in which you might have the experience you want and need.

Not all trances will be exceptional or productive, so if you have a trance in which nothing seems to happen, this is okay. You might also not 'see' things in trance (I don't), and this is completely fine. I try to use language that is inclusive and trauma-informed.

You can choose to record this trance ahead of time to help you settle in or you can read it a few times to lead yourself in the process. You might also want to share this with a friend or partner who might be willing to read the words to you.

To start, it will help to find a comfortable position in a place where you will not be interrupted. You can choose to lay down or sit upright or even walk around. All of these will work for the trance, and you can adjust as needed during the trance. The goal is to be comfortable and present, without falling asleep. But if you do fall asleep, this is not a problem. The words will likely still get into your subconscious, and you might find messages from your trance in later dreams.

Once you have found a comfortable position, allow your eyes to close or half close, if that feels good. You can also choose to have your eyes open and look at something that allows you to remain focused and present, e.g., a candle, a comforting picture or plant, etc.

As you find this place of settling, I invite you to notice your breath. You don't have to change it or fix it. You don't have to make it deeper or shallower. Just notice where your breath is and how that feels for you. You may notice you want to change it to help you feel more relaxed, but there is no pressure to change anything.

Your body can easily settle into the space you're in. To help it settle even further, I invite you to think about your body and how it has helped you today. You might think about how you have moved or how you have stayed still. You might think about the way your body has supported you in your life and how it continues to help you navigate the world.

Allow your awareness of your body to settle on your feet and ankles. What do you notice here? There is no need to change or fix anything; just notice what lives here right now. And if there is anything that doesn't need to be here, allow it to sink, drop, and fall away.

(Wait about 10 beats.)

You can then allow your awareness of your body to settle on your calves and knees and all along your thighs, back and front. What do you notice here? There is no need to change or fix anything; just notice what lives here right now. And if there is anything that doesn't need to be here, allow it to sink, drop, and fall away.

(Wait about 10 beats.)

Allow your awareness to travel to the space of your pelvic bowl, maybe even swirl around in this space. What do you notice here? There is no need to change or fix anything; just notice what lives here right now. And if there is anything that doesn't need to be here, allow it to sink, drop, and fall away.

(Wait about 10 beats.)

Invite your awareness to travel up to the space of your intestines and will, your solar plexus and the place of digestion. What do you notice here? There is no need to change or fix anything; just notice what lives here right now. And if there is anything that doesn't need to be here, allow it to sink, drop, and fall away.

(Wait about 10 beats.)

Allow your awareness to travel to your ribs and lungs, and to your courageous heart. What do you notice here? There is no need to change or fix anything; just notice what lives here right now. And if there is anything that doesn't need to be here right now, allow it to sink, drop, and fall away.

(Wait about 10 beats.)

Next, invite your awareness to travel to your shoulders and down the length of each arm – from shoulder to elbow to wrist, fingers, and thumbs. What do you notice here? There is no need to change or fix anything; just notice what lives here right now. And if there is *anything that doesn't need to be here right now, allow it to sink, drop, and fall away.*

(Wait about 10 beats.)

Ask your awareness to travel to your neck and jaw, maybe giving it a little shake to release any tension. Allow your awareness to travel the space of your eyes and mouth to your forehead, and all the way to the top of your head and the space that was soft when you were born. What do you notice here? There is no need to change or fix, just notice what lives here. And if there is anything that doesn't need to be here right now, allow it to sink, drop, and fall away.

(Wait about 10 beats.)

Maybe just one more time, scan your body to see if there are any lingering things that need to drop, sink, and fall away.

(Wait about 10 beats.)

Once you feel present and grounded and safe and calm, from the top of your head, I invite you to expand that awareness. You can choose to open your magickal or witchy eye, or you might roll out your awareness like a blanket from the top of your head out to all of the spaces to the horizon. You get to choose what makes sense to you. The goal is to open and widen out so you can tap into something bigger, something wiser inside of you.

As you begin to understand and know your wisdom, you might notice a path is waiting for you. What does this path look like? What does it feel like? What is the smell and the temperature? What direction is it moving? How does it curve? Is it easy to walk on? Do you need to float above it? Follow this path that knows your name and wants you to take a journey that will lead you to answers you are seeking.

The path goes on for as long as it needs to and it might take you through forests, along water, to a temple, or to many other possible perfect places. All these journeys are for you to enjoy and explore. Take your time as you travel, knowing every step is the right step and every step is the one that gets you closer to where you need to go right now.

After a while, you might find yourself at a clearing or a destination where a figure waits for you. They might become clear to your eyes or mind, or they might remain in shadow, but this figure feels like someone who welcomes you. It is Hestia.

I invite you to go to Her to see what She might have to share and say, to see what She might have to offer to you right now. You also might have questions to ask, or you might just sit in silence with Her to see what happens. There is no wrong choice. This time with Hestia is yours.

(Wait a few minutes.)

Unfortunately, we can't stay in these magickal spaces for long, though we can always return. Take a few moments to finish any conversation or interaction with Hestia, maybe even offering gratitude or a gift for in a few moments, we will return.

(Wait a minute.)

It is now time to return to where you came from, so you can thank Hestia or whatever being greeted you. Make the turn toward the path that led you here, and you might notice it is more familiar and easier to traverse. You make your way back easily and quickly, finding yourself at the place you began.

From this place, begin to roll in or call back the widened awareness. Allow it to curl and fold back into your body, where it belongs. And return to the top of your head and to your forehead, eyes, mouth, and throat, back back.

Return to your neck and shoulders and arms, back back.
Return to your courageous heart, lungs, and ribs, back back.
Return to your intestines and will and digestion, back back.
Return to your pelvic bowl, back back.
Return to your thighs, knees, and calves, back back.
And back to your toes and feet, back back.

Open your eyes if they have been closed. Say your name out loud a few times. Think about what is on the table closest to your bed. Drink some water. You might want to journal about your experience to capture what you experienced.

If you're not sure what to write down, here are some helpful prompts:

- What questions did I want to ask?
- What answers did I receive?
- What symbols or impressions did I experience?
- What emotions did I feel during the experience?
- How do I feel now that the experience is over?

I encourage everyone who wants to work with a godd to travel to them to ask questions and to be with them on a regular basis. This helps you build a relationship based on multiple experiences and can give you a sense of who they are when they encounter you too.

Chapter 2

The Birth & Family of Hestia

But Rhea was subject in love to Kronos (Cronus) and bare splendid children, Hestia, Demeter, and gold-shod Hera and strong Haides...and the loud-crashing Earth-Shaker [Poseidon], and wise Zeus...These great Kronos swallowed as each came forth from the womb to his mother's knees...Therefore he kept no blind outlook, but watched and swallowed down his children...As the years rolled on, great Kronos the wily was beguiled by the deep suggestions of Gaia (Gaea, the Earth), and brought up again his offspring, vanquished by the arts and might of his own son, and he vomited up first the stone which he had swallowed last.

Hesiod, Theogony 453 ff, trans.

Evelyn-White

Born of Cronos and Rhea, Hestia is the sister of Zeus, Poseidon, Hera, Demeter, and Hades. But Cronos learned from Gaia and Uranus that Cronos' children would overthrow him, just as Cronos had done to his own father. As the translations indicate, these children were born into the world, only to be swallowed up by Cronos almost immediately. Hestia was the first to be swallowed up. And Zeus was the only one who was spared, as Rhea helped him avoid that fate by wrapping a stone in a blanket and tricking Cronos into thinking he was swallowing Zeus.

During the War of the Titans, Zeus came back for his siblings and released them from this fate, with Hestia being released last.

When Zeus was grown, he engaged Okeanos' (Oceanus')
daughter Metis as a colleague. She gave Kronos a drug, by
which he was forced to vomit forth first the stone and then
the children he had swallowed. Pseudo-Apollodorus,
Bibliotheca 1.2.1 (trans. Aldrich) (Greek mythographer
C2nd A.D.)

Because of this unique birth, Hestia was both the oldest and
the youngest daughter. Eventually, Hestia and Her siblings
would fight in the War of the Titans and help to secure control
from their father. Many of these siblings became a part of the 12
Olympians, overseeing the matters of Greece.

Hestia's Siblings

Cronus married his sister Rhea, to whom the oak is sacred.
But it was prophesied by Mother Earth, and by his dying
father, Uranus, that one of his own sons would dethrone
him. Every year, therefore, he swallowed his children,
whom Rhea bore him: first Hestia, then Demeter and
Hera, then Hades, then Poseidon (Graves 39).

For those unfamiliar, I offer a small description of Hestia's
siblings:

Zeus – ruler of Olympus, married to Hera, god of sky and
lightning.
Poseidon – ruler of the sea and storms, often carries a
trident.
Hera – goddess of marriage and childbirth, wife of Zeus.
Demeter – goddess of the harvest and agriculture, mother
of Persephone.
Hades – god of the dead and kind of the underworld.

These siblings were different in nature than Hestia, as you will learn in the next chapter. She who is the hearth was not interested in the power grabs Her brothers and sisters were.

[H]aving established his worship throughout the world, Dionysus ascended to Heaven, and now sits at the right hand of Zeus as one of the Twelve Great Ones. The self-effacing goddess Hestia resigned her seat at the high table in his favour; glad of any excuse to escape the jealous wranglings of her family, and knowing that she could always count on a quiet welcome in any Greek city which it might please her to visit (Graves 106).

Chapter 3

Hestia Stories & Myths

Gentle and peace-loving, Hestia doesn't appear in too many myths...Plato says that this is because she has to remain in the house of the gods, all alone, tending the eternal celestial fire even when all the other Olympians ritually pass in processions through heavens. This is both her privilege and her predicament. Consequently, Hestia's only manifestation among humans was the crackling of the fire. Aristotle says that it is the sound of the goddess laughing.[5]

For the potential concern about Hestia not having a lot of stories, it seems She was present during some important parts of Greek mythology, including the War of the Titans. In addition, She still acted as one of the Olympians on Mount Olympus, so Her role was important, even if it was quiet in texts.

War of the Titans

The War of the Titans, or Titanomachy, a ten-year battle in Ancient Thessaly, began when Cronos sought out to overthrow his own father, Uranus, with the help of his mother Gaia. Gaia tried to get Her other children to castrate Uranus, but only Cronos would take on the task. But in this conflict, Uranus cursed his son to the same fate that he had endured. And, of course, this is why Cronos decided to eat his children, for his own protection.

Once Hestia and Her siblings (Poseidon, Hera, Demeter, and Hades) were freed from the stomach of Cronos, they joined Zeus in fighting against Cronos. After many years, the siblings won and established their power at Mount Olympus. Zeus married Hera, and Zeus started to assign different domains to his siblings. Zeus gained control of the sky, Poseidon of the water, and Hades of the underworld.

Another part of the story sees Hestia put into an interesting position, where Hera wanted to dethrone Zeus during this War. Hera went to Apollo, Poseidon, and Athena for help, but they all wanted their own power instead of siding with Hera. In some versions of the story, so committed to her task, Hera gave Zeus a potion to make him fall asleep, giving her time to figure out how to complete the coup. In Graves' retelling:

> A time came when Zeus' pride and petulance became so intolerable that Hera, Poseidon, Apollo, and all the other Olympians, except Hestia, surrounded him suddenly as he lay asleep on his couch and bound him with rawhide thongs, knotted into a thousand knots, so that he could not move. He threatened them with instant death, but they had placed his thunderbolt out of reach and laughed insultingly at him (53-54).

Hestia did not support this happening and didn't participate, instead She stayed far away from Her siblings during this time. Zeus was freed eventually and punished Hera, Poseidon, and Apollo for their roles in the coup. And Hestia was spared.

Hestia's Chosen Virginity

Nor yet does the pure maiden Hestia love Aphrodite's works. She was the first-born child of wily Cronos and youngest too, by will of Zeus who holds the aegis, —a queenly maid whom both Poseidon and Apollo sought to wed. But she was wholly unwilling, nay, stubbornly refused; and touching the head of father Zeus who holds the aegis, she, that fair goddess, swear a great oath which has in truth been fulfilled, that she would be a maiden all her days. So Zeus the Father gave her a high honor instead of marriage, and she has her place in the midst of the house and has the richest portion. In all the temples of the gods she has a share of honor, and among all mortal men she is chief of the goddesses. The Homeric Hymns and Homerica. English Translation by Hugh G. Evelyn-White

Hestia refused to marry Apollo or Her brother Poseidon, instead going to Zeus and touching his head to swear an oath that She would be a virgin for the span of Her life. In this passage, a reader is reminded that while She is not the partner of anyone, She has the most important part in a household and the richest of the offerings, so She is not suffering from any lack of attention or reverence.

Some scholars note that Hestia's decision to remain a virgin might be an act of trying to prevent conflict among the godds. After all, choosing between those two suitors would cause turmoil no matter who She chose. In Her decision, She made a sacrifice for the greater good, and some note that Zeus was moved by his sister's decision.[6]

Hestia & the Donkey

One of the few stories of Hestia that was written by the Roman poet Ovid speaks of a time when Hestia was sleeping in the woods at a feast. While She was asleep the vegetation and fertility godd, Priapus tried to rape Her, but a donkey saw what was happening and made a noise that woke the goddess up. The guests chased the drunken godd away. When the other godds found out what had happened, Priapus was banished to the forest and away from Mount Olympus.

Should I omit or recount your shame, red Priapus? It is a very playful, tiny tale. Coroneted Cybele [Rhea], with her crown of turrets, invites the eternal gods to her feast. She invites, too, Satyri (Satyrs) and Nymphae (Nymphs), Rural-Spirits (Rustica Numina); Silenus is present, uninvited. It's not allowed and too long to narrate the gods' banquet: night was consumed with much wine. Some blindly stroll shadowy Ida's dells, or lie down and rest their bodies in the soft grass. Others play or are clasped by sleep; or link their arms and thump the green earth in triple quick step. Vesta [Hestia] lies down and takes a quiet, carefree nap, just as she was, her head pillowed by turf. But the red saviour of gardens [Priapos] prowls for Nymphai and goddesses, and wanders back and forth. He spots Vesta. It's unclear if he thought she was a Nympha or knew it was Vesta. He claims ignorance. He conceives a vile hope and tires to steal upon her, walking on tiptoe, as his heart flutters. By chance old Silenus had left the donkey he came on by a gently burbling stream. The long Hellespont's god was getting started, when it bellowed an untimely bray. The goddess stars up, frightened by the noise. The whole crowd fly to her; the god flees through hostile hands. Ovid, Fasti 6. 319 ff (trans. Boyle) (Roman poetry C1st B.C. to C1st A.D.)

It is said that this story is why donkeys are decorated in garland during Hestia's feast day, possibly June 8 or 9, but this is not definitive.

Practice: Working with the Stories of Hestia

One of my favorite practices with godds is to look at their stories from different angles and viewpoints. For example, looking at the story of the War of the Titans allows one to see the many angles of siblings and their motivations. This can also give insight into Hestia and why She is the peacemaker and why She doesn't have more space in the myths.

While working with the stories is something that is a practice of possibility and not of trying to prove something is true or not, a practice of considering multiple sides is essential in relationship-building. Not only does this allow you to stay flexible in terms of interpretation, but it also expands understanding and reduces judgment.

Here are a few quick things you can do:

- Tell each story through the eyes of one character.
- Consider the emotions and motivations of this character.
- Notice how your experience of other characters in the stories shifts (or not).
- Try to find reasonable explanations for the choices of each character.

There is a practice I've done in classes to work with this process. One is called Theater of the Oppressed[7], which was created by Augusto Boal. In this practice, I get groups of students to take on the role of each character, acting out what is found in a text. But at some point, there is a moment to freeze, shift the story to something that isn't in the book, and see what might happen when you embody the character's motivations.

For example, a group might have Zeus, Hera, and Hestia in it. Each of these characters have different motivations, Zeus is upset that Hera tried to overthrow him, but also continues to be married to Her, so does this inform his ongoing infidelity? What might Hestia have to say to Her brother about that?

Even if you don't have a group of people, journal about what the individuals in stories might also have done in the stories, what other choices they could have made. The more you do this, the more you can begin to also see the characters as complex, nuanced, and more human-like.

Chapter 4

Worshiping Hestia

Oxford Languages defines 'worship' as the "feeling or expression of reverence and adoration for a deity" or "the acts or rites that make up a formal expression of reverence for a deity; a religious ceremony or ceremonies" or adoration or devotion comparable to religious homage, shown toward a person or principle."

Hestia is often seen as being worshiped alongside Apollo and Poseidon, which is even mentioned at the Temple of Delphi. The fact that this happened seems to indicate that Hestia was aware these two wanted to have Her hand in marriage.[8] But as She refused, I wonder if this worship was a way to keep things peaceful and balanced.

'Ancient' Worship & Domestic Life

While the idea of worship seems complicated and even dull, Hestia was worshiped in the mundane, but essential, moments of life. She would witness the preparation of meals by families at the hearth, which was the religious focus of a home and the place of offerings and sacrifices.

But the hearth was not just for cooking. It was also a place for rituals around birth and death. In celebration of a birth, a baby would be carried around the hearth and new household members would be bathed in nuts and figs while sitting in front of the hearth as Hestia's blessings. When someone died, the fire would be put out and then lit again to honor the death.

Women were the ones who typically watched over the fire, ensuring it never went out. If the fire did go out for some reason, it was thought this was a sign that Hestia removed Her favor from the family. To light the fire again, the family could go to the public hearth to get an ember.

Hamilton writes that every meal began and ended with an offering to Hestia (37):

> Hestia, in all dwellings of men and immortals
> Yours is the highest honor, the sweet wine offered
> First and last at the feast, poured out to you duly.
> Never without you can gods or mortals hold banquet.

The everyday life of the Greeks centered on family and togetherness, not only for nostalgia, but also for survival. The fire was necessary for food and life. Hestia was at the center of that, and some have even noted that the very idea of having a hearth in a home comes from Her worship.

Traditions with Hestia

Birth and Marriage

> One of the most characteristic manifestations of Greek sacred space was the hestia, the circular hearth which formed the center of the house and around which various rites such as marriage and the deposition of the infant took place. The hestia was also the seat of the goddess Hestia who accordingly symbolized the solidity and immobility of the cosmos as well as the centeredness of enclosed, domestic space. Not only did the hestia anchor the house to the earth but through the roof opening over it the god's portion of the meals cooked on the hearth rose to the world above.[9]

People gave birth and were married around the hearth, and as Hestia is the hearth, She witnessed these rites and blessed them with Her presence.

> .... Hestia came to represent the sacred bond of family (as understood by its members). To that end, 'children, brides, and slaves were formally accepted into the family by being led to or around the hearth, often in a shower of dried fruits and nuts, a ceremony no doubt performed by the father with all the other family members present.'[10]

Again, we see that those who entered into a family (willingly or not) were taken to the hearth to be blessed in this transition.

There is also the celebration of Amphidromia,[11] when a child would be presented to Hestia five to seven days after their birth, as many children died before they were seven days old. The child would be carried around Hestia's hearth to be presented to the gods of the house and the family. Members of the family often brought gifts, and the house would be decorated with olive branches if the child was a boy and with wool garlands if the child was a girl.

Mourning

> The Hestia of the home was always extinguished on an occasion of mourning, if the latter signified at the same time the end of a household, the death of a family, the abandonment of a location, and the dispersion of those who had formerly constituted the household (Paris 168).

Since the hearth is the embodiment of the health of a family, when someone died, it makes sense that the flame was put out then too. The flame would be lit again after a period of mourning, but if the person was the end of the family or the home was no longer going to be lived in by that family, the flame was put out for good.

Hestia could go to a new place, but Her part in that family would be complete.

Public Worship

According to Monaghan's scholarship, "There were never statues of this most ancient Greek goddess, for she took no human form" (152). Most sources I reviewed noted there were no temples to Hestia, though there were plenty of places where She was honored.

However, Hestia's fires would be lit in homes as well as in places near meeting halls.

Besides individual homes, Hestia was particularly associated with the prytaneion and bouleuterion, the symbolic centre of a town or city where civic functions were held and the business of local government was carried out. Here there was usually a hearth which was a tradition dating back to Mycenaean Greece when the king's throne and reception room in his palace, the megaron, had a large hearth. The later town's hearth was continuously maintained by the community, typically by unmarried women selected for that purpose. The goddess received sacrifices at this communal hearth each time a new magistrate began and ended their term of office and before council sessions. Curiously, following the failed invasion of Greece by the Persians in the 5th century BCE, Delphi – in many ways the religious heart of the Greek city-states – ordered that all communal hearths be extinguished because they were now considered impure.

The hearths were then relit using purified flames taken from the hearth at Delphi.[12]

Ancient worshipers, known as theopropoi, would come to Delphi and expect to speak with Pythia, the Oracle. After preparing their bodies and minds for this encounter, they would enter via the east steps into the temple, which was surrounded by pillars. This cellar area was where Hestia's hearth resided, and this is where the Eternal Flame of Greece burned (Goodrich 199).

Because of the lack of visual representation of Hestia, it is said that She resided in the flame itself, as a living flame.

There is evidence of some cults for Hestia in Attica at Piraeus, Eleusis, Halimos, and Krokonidai. At other cults in Kos and Kaukratis, women were not permitted to participate in the rituals to Hestia as She was so closely related to politics, which only men participated in.[13]

Traditional Sacrifices

Monaghan shares that offerings to Hestia might include the "first fruits, water, oil, wine and year-old cows" (152).

In writing about Hestia, She may not have a partner and She might not have a particular domain as Zeus bestowed amongst his brothers, but She was the one who received the first offerings from families and towns. Hestia was promised the fatty offerings in the hopes of keeping Her favor.

These sacrifices and offerings were thought to help Hestia continue to bless the family and the community. When these sacrifices were not granted, it might be possible that She could take away peace in public and domestic life.

Some sacrifices include the one-year-old cows of the family. And remember that Her flames were at the temples of all of the godds, so She would get all of the first sacrifices.

While we've talked about the ways in which sacrifice used to look, what is important to note today is the idea of 'sacrifice' is not something from ancient Greece. The word 'sacrifice' is actually Latin and means to basically give something to a godd. According to Sarah Hitch:

> Often this ritual [sacrifice], because the term "sacrifice" is a modern construct largely colored by Roman and Christian perceptions, eludes interpretation. The Greeks themselves had no words for "religion" or "ritual," both terms derived from Latin. Drawing on our own cultural experience, we may be tempted to apply retroactively concepts of "sacred" and "secular," the former part of "religion" or "religious worship," but these words imply a distinction that would have been meaningless in antiquity. There were also many types of offerings to the gods, a spectrum of actions with variations in meaning and context, perceived by ancient Greeks as obligatory, both as acts of devotion and as symbols of membership in a community.[14]

With this information, it becomes clear that what people have read and translated from ancient Greek may not have had the same meaning as they have been given. When I read about the possibility of sacrifices being more about being devoted to the godds and about proving commitment to a community, these practices become more approachable.

Hitch goes on to talk about there haven't been studies of animal sacrifice, at the time of Her writing, but there has been more research into oath making, supplication, and burial practices. What might be surmised at this point is that the description of animal sacrifices might be more for poetic technique and to prove just how devoted the characters were to the godds.

Modern Worship Ideas

Bringing Hestia into the modern world can be as simple as gathering around a fire or in a stove, oven, or microwave. To this day, households consider their kitchen to be the central meeting place of families and communities. When inviting people over, I know people tend to congregate in the kitchen, even if no one is cooking.

If you want to invite Hestia's blessings, it makes sense to go to this place of the modern eternal flame. (And if you don't have access to a kitchen, a candle or representation of a fire will work well too.)

Cooking

Making food for others is an act of service and love. When people come together, no matter the occasion or mood, food often arrives as the focal point. People bring what they can share and eat together in solidarity and community. Even if you're not a cook or comfortable in a kitchen, you can bring Hestia into your life with smaller acts of cooking. You can become a hearth witch along the way.

I recommend dedicating time to Hestia whenever you are in the kitchen to make something. You might even take a small portion of the meal and put it on an altar to Her. This way, She gets the first offering, and you honor Her presence.

- **Make a meal for Her –** You can look for recipes that you think She might enjoy and make them in honor of Her. This doesn't need to be complicated or elaborate, but you can choose to make things that will call Her presence to you. This might include bread or soup or things that can tend to the needs of a family – even if it's just you.
- **Make a meal for community** – Whenever you gather with friends and family, you can dedicate the meal in Her

honor. This intention doesn't even need to be shared with the group. The act of service aligns with Hestia's energy and magick. If possible, you might want to step into a kitchen that makes food for those who are unhoused and need a hot meal. Hestia is in the spaces of creating and offering blessings of nourishment to keep communities and families healthy and whole.

- **Make family recipes** – A magick that I like to invoke with Hestia's support is related to my ancestors and the meals they would prepare. I am lucky to have recipe books from a few generations of my family, and while I do not think of myself as a cook, I do know how to make a few of these recipes in my family's honor. To celebrate Hestia, I make a fruit bread that has been made for decades. And I hope to expand into other recipes that were made so many times, the pages are almost translucent from the cooking oil stains. When you make the food of your family and your lineage, you call back into your space the value of your domestic life. If this doesn't appeal to you, you could also create a space in which you choose the new recipes to start your own traditions.

- **Use what you have** – When working with Hestia, I wonder about making things from what I already have in the cupboards. Instead of trying to buy all new things or trying to pick up a few items that you don't need every day, see what you can make from the bounty that is already around you.

- **Try new recipes** – Because there are so very many opportunities to feed people, you can work with Hestia as you try new recipes. These might be recommended from people you know, or they might be recipes you just want to try because they're something new. You can create magickal space when you make this food and invoke Hestia into the room as an ally.

Hestia can not only be an ally for trying new things, but you might also call on Her before you cook anything to show your gratitude. She can remind you of the ways you are blessed to have what you have, even if it isn't a lot. Starting any cooking with a 'thank you' to Hestia can also set the tone of calm and ease, just as She would have been in the kitchens of anyone who called Her name.

Cleaning

But cooking isn't the only domestic activity that relates to Hestia. Think about the hearth and how it needs to be tended. While you will not be tending a flame these days, you might choose to tend to a place, your home, or a location you call home. By showing reverence to your living space, you can honor Hestia's energy for creating the best spaces for community to thrive.

This isn't going to be a section that explains how to clean, nor is it going to be a place to outline how to keep everything pristine; rather, Hestia brings forward the energy of tending to the home. And your version of tending might look very different from mine.

Cleaning can entail physical and energetic modalities, depending on what you need in your home to feel safe and secure. I like to blend the practices of cleaning surfaces with removing unwanted or stuck energy. This can look like moving around my space to put back any items that have wandered away from where they are often stored. At that point, I might vacuum or sweep the floors. (I have cats and litter is always and forever everywhere.) Again, this doesn't feel like a chore, but it helps to remind yourself this is an act of service to your space, the space that holds you.

Some might want to dust or wipe down surfaces next or make the bed. You can choose to clean in the way that makes the most sense to you. I know there are certain things that make my space feel well-tended, but feel free to add your own ideas.

- Fresh sheets and my bed made.
- Clean bathroom sinks.
- Lighting some incense.
- Scrubbing the kitchen sink.
- Straightening up my altars or books.
- Removing old offerings from around deities or other places.
- Sweeping around the outside of my door.
- Wiping down mirrors and windows.
- Taking out the trash and recycling.

As a devotional practice to Hestia, you might find a time during the week where you can focus on cleaning and nothing else. You can start the practice in gratitude to Hestia and to the blessings you have witnessed and received. From there, you might say aloud or in your head what you are doing and how this is in service to this godd.

Thank you, Hestia, for the blessings of this week, of the way you helped my family stay close and committed to each other. In service to you and myself, I will spend an hour cleaning the kitchen and the shared spaces in my home. As I do this, I ask for your blessing and your guidance, as you know the value and honor of service.

And this doesn't have to be an hour-long practice either. You might choose to clean or cook for a few minutes a day. You might choose to spend an entire day. It's up to you what feels like devotion to you within your relationship to Hestia.

Unseen Service / Modern Sacrifice

For many, there is a complexity in the idea of service and sacrifice. There are some who have taught me that service is noble and something to be prioritized. I have seen people who serve others more than they honor themselves, and often society praises this approach. In other settings, I have seen people refuse to regard the idea of sacrifice. In those places, I have heard people talk about how they don't want to give up things anymore, as they equate sacrifice with abandonment of needs or desires. And this is a nuanced conversation, which has points on all sides.

Service to community is something that is done for the good of the group. It is not something done for the recognition or another reward, outside of helping the community. I do believe and think it is reasonable to know your service level should align with your energy, your time, and your resources. To go beyond this is to do yourself a disservice.

I also think of sacrifice as something honorable. In every moment, there are things we give up in order to do other things. For example, right now, I could be out on a walk, but I am sitting on my couch with my laptop, writing this. I have decided that writing is what I want to do and to do that, I need to be here instead of outside. Look at Hestia and what She sacrificed to keep the peace in Her family, as another example.

What I want to say is that working with Hestia requires a close examination of the service you can offer to your community. What can you do to help? What talents can you share? What resources can you offer?

- Money
- Time
- Attention
- Support

You may even want to step back from concrete examples and think about what you have available to you right now.

When you get a sense of this and work to serve others within those parameters, you will be able to offer support without burning out.

Of course, there are likely going to be times when you will go beyond your limits to help another. How many of us have had a sick relative or pet? It might be the right thing to stretch yourself a little further than you can or want to – because it's what the community and your loved ones need.

The question of giving too much or too little is mitigated when we are honest with ourselves about what we CAN do. When we also communicate these limits with others, it becomes easier for everyone to know what might be possible and where additional support may be needed. You can't do everything, and you shouldn't.

While it's true that service will not always feel good and it may often go unrecognized, Hestia knows and sees it.

Here are some small ways you can add acts of service into your life without anyone necessarily seeing them.

- Pick up trash when you're out on a walk.
- Sweep your neighbor's sidewalk.
- Donate to causes that need help.
- Pay attention to your friend who is going through a hard time; listen to them and validate their experience.
- Smile at someone.
- Send a friend a card if they're going through a hard time.

I invite you to add to this list as you like. What small things can you do to help others feel supported? How can you add energy and life to your community without spending hours away from your own life? There are many ways to create goodwill and blessings.

And just as Hestia didn't ask for recognition, I invite you to do these things without wondering if anyone liked them or noticed them. There is power and magick in these actions. Step in where you can when you can. Service is not always attention-grabbing, but it will be noticed.

Community Tending / Volunteering

Whenever I think of Hestia, I think of the ways in which we might help others. I think of how modern society seems to have structured things to be less focused on togetherness and more on separateness. Families have their own homes versus sharing with other generations. Children are pressured to move out and be on their own, instead of having roommates. Instead of sharing our resources, capitalism tells us to get our own car, our own TV, etc.

Bringing ourselves together again is the magick of Hestia. Coming together in care and concern is not only a magick of connection, but also a magick of sustainability. We are not supposed to do all of the things in our lives on our own. We are supposed to do things in community. We're supposed to heal in community and learn in community. We are supposed to be together when things are hard so we can support each other.

We are meant to tend to each other. We can do this by communicating more with the people in our local area. This might include friends and family, but it also may not. We can start to get involved in knowing how our neighbors are and what they might need. We can check on each other and we can make sure everyone knows they have someone to turn to if there is an emergency or a need.

This can extend to those who might need support in other ways. I encourage you to investigate local volunteering groups to see what the needs are and how you might be able to support them. In doing so, you create a stronger connection of community, and light a flame that will keep people warm and nourished. Hestia's work is about remembering each other no matter where we are and what is happening.

You can also choose to do this service and work as a group. Perhaps you and your friends can help with a local environmental clean-up or you might choose to help in a soup kitchen or other organization. Come together to help others, and this will ensure everyone has someone.

Hestia Blessing for the Home

To help you sink into the work of Hestia and to call Her more strongly into your space and actions, here is a blessing that can be altered as you see fit. I also invite you to write your own prayers and blessings to Hestia as offerings.

Sweet and serene Hestia,
Goddess of Hearth and Flame,
I honor your wisdom and kindness,
I invite your grace into this home,
Into this space where fire warms and provides,
Into this space where family of blood and choice gather,
Into this heart where community and connection begins.

Hestia, first and last born,
You do not need praise, but your actions are praiseworthy,
You who can pause and reflect before acting,
I honor your willingness to restore peace,
I honor the magick of creating meeting places,
I honor the spell of your offerings,
The ones that are first above all,
And given before anyone else.

Hestia, bless this place with your crackling flame,
Let these walls hold the complexity of community,
And the impulsivity of humans,
Let this space be one of learning and loving,

Let this place be one of service and humility,
I ask that you bless every attempt at connection
And every conflict that arises, as they do,
Because coming together is not always about quiet,
Sometimes we need to speak our truths
And know we will still be welcomed.

Hestia, bless this home with belonging,
With the true knowing of how we can all arrive as ourselves.
Bless us with curiosity to listen to understand,
Even when we do not agree.

Hestia, in all days and these days,
You are welcome in the fires of our hearts.

Hail Hestia!

Modern Sacrifices

When thinking about the idea of giving something to the godds,
our services might be the thing that holds value the most. After
all, the time and energy we give to these acts can be a reciprocal
act. In response to what we have been given by Hestia, we give
what we can, when we can.

You might also choose to expand your sacrifice practices
to the modern world by thinking about the things that honor
Hestia well. And while the slight charge of the word 'sacrifice'
might seem out of alignment with these suggestions, remember
the definition being something that is given into the hands of
the godds.

Burning of local herbs – The word 'thuein' or 'thysia' means to
make smoke and is thought to be related to sending messages
up to the godds of Olympus.[15] For a sacrifice, you might light a

hearth and burn herbs to send your honor to the godds. This can be a practice for certain times, or it might be daily, depending on what Hestia might ask of you.

Donation of food – For those who might bake or cook, the donation of food that is prepared by your hands would be a lovely sacrifice. Not only does this give something back to those in your community who might need more, but it also allows you to use the hearth (literally or figuratively) to bless the food before it travels onto its final destination. You can also find local shelters or centers that cook food for those in need, and you can donate your talents in cooking and preparation.

Giving of time and energy – While mentioned already, it cannot be stated enough that donating your time and energy is a sacrifice you can make to godds. Hestia asks that people come together in community to support each other, and it takes many hands to come together to support each other. By providing what you can, you are adding to the fire of the hearth. In doing so, the community continues to thrive, and everyone can tend to the emerging needs of individuals.

One of the things I like to remember when I am deciding on an appropriate sacrifice is how it reflects my intention. If I have been given or shown something amazing by Hestia, the sacrifice I want to offer in return should be equally weighted. To me, this means my sacrifice needs to be something I don't necessarily WANT to give up, but that I NEED to give up. It should be a little painful to release that sacrifice because part of me is bound up in it.

Now, this doesn't mean you need to give hours of your time and resources, become a burnt out worshiper and then you are Hestia's favorite. Instead, you want to think about what you can offer up that has true meaning. Because when something has meaning to you, it will mean more to the godds.

Hearth Magick

A much more common practice of working with Hestia in reverence is hearth magick, which has a few different definitions. The way I've seen hearth magick happen is the coming together of a group to cook together. These groups have made meals together, tinctures together, candles together, etc. What you want to have in your hearth is up to you, but here's an idea to help you get started.

If you already have a group of friends who like to cook together, this hearth magick can be as easy as setting up a day when you all bring something to cook together. Or you might have a few friends all cook different things at the same time, and then share what you have made with everyone. This way, you have multiple meals created at one time, celebrating the vibrancy of the hearth, as well as the skills of the people, and the blessings of Hestia.

Or you can have a group of friends focus on one hearth task per meeting. For example, if one person is really interested in making bath salts, then you can all come together to make them together. And the next time you meet, someone might share their favorite pie recipe. The idea is to come together, cultivating community and teaching hearth skills so everyone can expand their abilities. The more you do this, the more you will be able to support yourself and others in your community.

It can also be helpful to call around to volunteer organizations to see how you might be able to help. If there is a need for holiday foods during a certain time of year, then you might be able to get a group together to make those foods. You may also find out that a certain group wants to fundraise but needs baked goods to do so.

Hearth magick can also be a place to share natural medicines, assuming you have practice and experience making them. Together, you can learn how to make tinctures and concoctions that might help with immune system support or calm coughs. Or you might come together to make tea blends or natural smoking blends. By sharing your knowledge and ingredients, you are supporting the ongoing hearth magick that is mutual aid and community care in action.

I have a friend who gathers with others every year to make tamales. It's a family tradition for her, and She invites people over to teach them how to make them. Everyone brings something to add and is shown how to participate in the building of the tamales, step-by-step. In the end, there is laughter, joy, and a lot of food to share. People go home with meat or vegetarian tamales, as well as a positive memory of the community's ability to come together to support each other well.

Chapter 5

Hestia & the Hearth

Hestia as earth means that she is the matrix, the material, the sine qua non of all differentiation, of self-realization, without which spirit remains suspended and never comes down.... The hearth altar originally signified the energy of 'the almost irresistible compulsion and urge to become what one is, just as every organism is driven to assume the form that is characteristic of its nature.' Thus, the ideas of the circle and of original materia (the earth) help explain why Hesiod says she was the first born; she is the ground of being (Demetrakopoulos 72-73).

The ongoing presence of Hestia in the ancient world reminds us today how important She was in everyday life. She may not have been embodied in the godds, but She was present in the human world. And even today, Hestia arrives in the modern culture at the Olympic Games, as the original athletes at Olympia would light their torches from Her sacred flame to bring back to their hometowns. This act of unity and sportsmanship was the essential of the original games, and a strong reminder of how Her hearth was not just a place, but also a practice.[16]

I like to think of the hearth as something that expands from not just one place, but from one goal: togetherness. While Hestia is the one who might personify the flame, She is a being who can be everywhere, all the time, because an idea cannot be contained. It can spread to those who want and need to hear it, it can spread like a very necessary wildfire.

The Importance of the Hearth

To banish or destroy a family is to drive out a hearth....
The ever-burning hearth in the temple at Delphi was
sometimes seen as the communal hearth for the whole of
Greece. The hearth is an offering place for libations and
small gifts of food; the beginning of the meal is marked
by these offerings being thrown into the fire. The proverb,
'Begin from the hearth,' therefore signifies a good and
sound beginning (Burkert 170).

The idea of the hearth being a starting point resonates for me.
After all, where we are nourished and fed is where life begins
and where it is supported. Without the fire of the sun or the fire
of the hearth, it would not be possible to support life.

The hearth was not only for life-sustaining, but also
community sustaining. If you look back to the original Olympic
Games, it is sometimes described as the Vestal Virgins lighting
the torch by using a parabolic mirror to focus the energy of the
sun onto the torch.[17]

But what happened when one of the ancient fires went
out? This seems to be a little harder of a question to answer.
In some writings, it is said that when a fire was not tended
and it went out, certain rituals needed to be performed to coax
the fire back. However, as there was not a word for 'ritual'
in ancient Greece, it seems that this might not be accurate.
One could also look back to the story of Prometheus and how
he stole fire from the godds, a story that might be used to
talk about what needed to happen to get fire.[18] The myth,
however, is not necessarily about actual fire, and probably
more about how Prometheus stole knowledge from the godds
for humankind. And the story of Prometheus didn't turn out
too well for him, as his punishment for stealing condemned

him to having his liver eaten each day by an eagle. But the liver would grow back each night, only to be eaten again the following day.

Even the vocabulary for hearth enunciated its religious aspects. The Mycenaean word for hearth was e-ka-ra, which later became ἐσχάρα in early Greek literature. Adrian Parvulescu has suggested that this is a combination of es and charan (in gratitude [to a divinity]), a reading that follows naturally with the religious interpretation of the hearth, though that etymology is not reliable. Nevertheless, fire is a natural element that evokes religious meaning: it has power both to destroy and to regenerate. It is an agent of change, as Heraclitus, philosopher and fire enthusiast, later emphasized. It both consumes noxious elements, as in cooking or disinfecting, and facilitates transformation, as in metallurgy or pottery craft. The protean form of fire and the metamorphic work that it performs naturally led its beneficiaries to identify it as a religious force. Early Greek hearths, therefore, in addition to providing a setting for practical and social activities, functioned in a ritual context.[19]

The hearth was designated as a palace for practical and spiritual connection. This was a place where people would gather to celebrate, but also to tend to the complexities of community. A hearth was the heart, and a place where things could be broken and fixed. Again and again. To me, this is the holiness of Hestia, the magick and the mystery of fire.

Even in ancient Greek times, Homer talked about how the lands were covered in wildfires, much like today. (At the time of writing this section, Greece was facing new wildfires.) The roaming peoples of the time wanted to convert the forested lands to grasslands to support cattle and livestock, shaping the ecology and the patterns of growth in the land today.[20]

Building a Modern Hearth

The figure known to the Greeks as Hestia provided the city with one means of exercising and building up its own autonomy. Her name was commonly understood to mean "fire," the fire in the hearth or the fire on the altar, which was connected both with eating and with sacrifice: with sacrifice because it marked out the fixed center of a cult, rooted in the earth yet at the same time a human construction, the work of an architect. But for this hearth or altar to become the Common Fire, Hestia Koinē, it was necessary for it to absorb the values developed from the idea of the equidistant center and focal point of fair distribution. Various practices and new liturgies, creating a whole new ceremonial, were evolved to proclaim the special powers of Hestia. (Detienne 62)

With this in mind, the hearth is clearly not just a place, but also a set of values. In this section, I offer two ways to build a modern hearth, and I invite you to feel into your own relationship to Hestia and your community to see what might work for you. Feel free to adjust anything I offer since your hearth is your hearth and needs to reflect what you know to be true about your community.

Altar Building: The Hearth You Build with Your Hands
For those who want to have a physical hearth, you can begin with what you already have in your home or other shared place. Look at your kitchen and/or your fireplace areas. With these in place, you can create altars of devotion or spaces where Hestia is welcome. I would encourage you to remove anything from

these spaces that isn't adding to the sacredness, and adding things that might encourage more reverence.

This might include some of the symbols and offerings of Hestia, for example. You can also include things that remind you of togetherness, e.g., family pictures. I would also include items related to my family of origin, including small trinkets that were given to me by my ancestors.

If you don't have a physical structure for your hearth, or you want to build another one, here are some suggestions:

- Use a row of candles to create an ongoing flame in a place dedicated to Hestia.
- Install an electric fireplace or hearth in the space you have for Hestia.
- Hang a picture of a hearth and create an altar beneath it to focus on the energy of Hestia.

I offer these simpler suggestions especially to families with animals and children who like to disrupt altars. You don't have to do things too extravagantly to make a space sacred. I also suggest putting a hearth in a closet or a cupboard if you need to hide it away from eyes that don't understand your practices.

Individual Practice:
The Hearth You Build with Your Heart

A hearth is not just a physical space you can touch; it's also the values and beliefs you want to hold in your community. How you define community is up to you, firstly. You might choose to include your family and friends in that grouping, or you might expand to something wider, like a coven, a spiritual tradition, a neighborhood, etc.

Who is not as important as why, in my opinion. What do you want your group to believe in and be accountable to? This requires sitting down with the group to answer those questions.

I suggest finding a list of values and then deciding which ones are the ones everyone can agree to as a group.

Values include things like accountability, beauty, compassion, courage, diversity, empathy, faith, freedom, gratitude, growth, health, honesty, integrity, justice, love, loyalty, optimism, peace, respect, sacrifice, etc. There are many lists of values available online and through education programs.

You can make this a fun activity, an act of collaboration with the support of Hestia by writing out the values you want to embody as a group, and then share with each other how you think these would look for you. If you were to embody integrity, what would that look like? How would someone know you were embodying this? Each person can go through their values with examples, and in the end, the values that seem to be most consistent among the group are likely the ones that will be agreed on.

Of course, your group gets to decide what makes the most sense to everyone and what works. You can also decide on a few values (less is often easier to manage at first), and then come back together in a certain period to decide if you need more – or less.

Values allow groups to return to what is important. If there is conflict, for example, it is easier to manage when you know you hold the same values as someone else. You can see they are trying to be in integrity, though they might be doing things in a way that is different from you. Or you might find out that people don't share the same values, which is another conversation that can be healing.

A hearth built with your hearts is one that will be able to navigate complicated situations, as there are so many of them in life. With shared values, you can also ask Hestia to bless these for your group and help you hold them well. It might be wise to light a candle for each value and keep these fires lit to show that the values are lighting the way as you move forward together.

Chapter 6

Symbols & Offerings

Hestia is represented as almost completely veiled with clothing, very straight, both imposing and discreet, and of a remarkable immobility. Seated or standing, she indicates no movement. Calm and dignity emanate from her (Paris 167).

While Hestia is not a presumptuous deity, She has been described as having a few symbols that can be used on altars or as offerings in Her name.

Fire

Fire with its multiple fascinations is present in almost every cult act of the Greeks. Sacrifices without fire are rare, conscious exceptions, and conversely there is rarely a fire without a sacrifice; the hearth, Hestia, is a goddess as well (Burkert 61).

Hestia is the hearth, and the hearth is Hestia. There is no separation, which is part of Her mystery and Her magick, but also makes the fire all the more important.

If Hestia's fire went out in the home or in a city of ancient Greece, the significance was tragic, and there were complex rituals for relighting it. Thus, when the Persians laid siege to Athens and extinguished the sacred fire, the Athenians, after defeating them, sent for fire from the great temple of Hestia at Delphi to re-kindle the fire of their own city (Paris 168).

Using fire on altars and in rituals with Hestia is a wise choice as it will call Her closer and Her energy closer to the work you might do.

Kettle / kettledrum

To further highlight the connection between Hestia and the hearth, a symbol for Her domestic role is the kettle or kettledrum.

Chaste-Tree

In some images of Hestia, of which there are few, She is seen holding a flowering branch, which scholars have speculated was chaste-tree[21]. This shrub is found in the Mediterranean and has violet/blue/white flowers and berries. As hinted at in its name, the chaste-tree is an anaphrodisiac, or a plant that might reduce feelings of attraction towards another. This aligns with the idea of Hestia being a virgin by choice and practice.

Figuring Out What to Offer

When starting to work with any deity, it is common to worry about offering the right or best offering. And since Hestia doesn't seem to have a lot of details about Her worship (since She was everywhere and always worshiped), it can seem daunting to choose something for this goddess.

The good news is that modern day practices offer the ability to have modern day solutions and answers to these questions. You don't have to have the right answer as you are making up a new answer for a new time. I would encourage you to think about what energies you appreciate about Hestia. Just as you might start to think about a new person in your life and what they might like, look to Her stories and to Her actions. What might She appreciate?

Some ideas I would offer include:

- Candles, either LED or with wicks.
- A cauldron or pot that might be used to cook food for a group.
- Lavender, as some sources point to this being a potentially sacred plant to Her.
- Olive branches for peace or other offerings related to peace.
- Pictures of happy families.
- An offering place with things you give to Her every day or every meal.
- A kettle of water that is boiled daily to be ready to welcome guests.

The longer you work with Hestia, the more you will be able to understand what She might enjoy or what She might enjoy more than other things. This is not a quiz or a test to offer a godd something; it is a gift. And sometimes it takes time to know what someone might like to receive. And the thought does count.

Chapter 7

Building Communities for Hestia

It is said that Hestia discovered how to construct
dwellings, and for this benefit she has a consecrated place
in every home among practically all peoples and receives
honors and sacrifices (Trzaskoma et al 98).

In many books about deities, one of the first things that's
suggested is to build an altar to the godd. It makes sense and it
certainly is what I would recommend (and have recommended),
but I also think Hestia is a little different.

There are altars and hearths in every home. I find these are
not just physical things or places, but also people who serve as
flames and places of worship. For me, Hestia is about creating
places at the hearth, places where people can be welcomed
and there they can be celebrated. In doing so, communities
are more connected and can be more sustainable in the long
term. Just as Hestia did what needed to be done to keep Her
family together, communities who support the larger needs of
the group will achieve their goals more easily and with less
conflict.

When we can begin to see the building of communities as
sacred work and as the building of altars for devotion, we don't
have to rely on certain things to be in place; everything we need
will already be there. The hope that building these physical
and non-physical altars to Hestia will provide the places for
communities to thrive.

The Importance of Recognition

For those who took part in public affairs, the politeumenoi, the sight of Hestia as herself and as represented by her statues, her agalmata, meant the city council, the Boulē, and also the place where the city's wealth was stored, the public treasury. For ordinary individuals, idiotai, Hestia represented the fact of living, life itself. And for a king, basileus, or a governor, archon, she was power, the dunamis of his own power, his own archē. The symbolism extended from the individual life of each separate household's hearth to the collective and public power personified by Hestia in the three manifestations of her single being: the city council, the public treasury, and the power of authority itself. The political Hestia, who was linked through her power to the life of each individual, established around her a space for the exercise of her autonomy, a space that took the material form of not only the Prytaneion, the home of the magistrates in power, but also her altar and her particular attributes. The "first" Greek democracies were set up under the sign of Hestia. (Detienne 63).

Recognizing the importance of this work can be motivating and sustaining for all that needs to come next. When I read this quote, I look at the way Hestia was instrumental in the construction of community and society. It might be said that She was the guide by which people learned to share power with each other and how they learned to come together in service of the greater good.

I begin with the conversation about recognition not to focus on the idea of being seen in the work of community, as Hestia isn't one for being in the spotlight, but I start here to show that this work is important. This work is everywhere that groups are, whether it is conscious or not. The more we can remember the importance of community, the more we can hold it with care and concern.

Once I was a part of a conversation with a community that was having troubles. There were arguments, disagreements, and hurt feelings all around the group. I sat with the group on a patio in the warmth of the midday sun and asked them what each person was feeling. Even though I'd talked to everyone ahead of time, it was clear people were in pain. While I had the job of helping to facilitate a conversation towards some sort of resolution, I realized the first thing that needed to be said was, "If no one cared, you wouldn't be in this much pain." When you do care and when you do want things to work out, even if you can't agree on how to move ahead, there is going to be discomfort and likely pain along the way. Recognizing this is a shared experience softens whatever comes next.

While it might seem like you can't agree on much, you can agree on one thing: this work of community is important. And this is where Hestia can guide the way.

Creating Sustainable Communities

The word, 'sustainability,' seems to be almost a buzzword in activism and business today. People talk about how to make things more sustainable when things aren't working well, when they're not happy, and when they're feeling burned out. To make something sustainable is to make it manageable and to make it something that can be supported where people are at, versus at a level of focus or a level of attention that is too demanding.

One of my goals in community is to prioritize sustainable practices, but what that looks like to me is not what it looks like to everyone else. So, with the guidance of Hestia, we need to begin with finding out what your group or your community wants. From there, you can create practices that will ensure folks feel supported and nurtured in being together.

Not only does this help make things sustainable, but it also promotes the practice of interdependence instead of overdependence or codependence. Healthy communities begin with understanding the needs of the whole and the needs of individuals. Just as Hestia made decisions based on keeping the peace, you too can make decisions based on the goal of effective interactions.

Group Practice: Defining Community & Value

As mentioned previously, finding your shared values can be a practice that helps define your community's needs and goals. You can use that earlier practice to start to identify your needs, and here is another practice you can use as a group.

To begin, you will need a facilitator or someone to guide the conversation. This is ideally someone who is not in the community since you want everyone's voices to be a part of this process. But if this needs to be a member of your group, that's okay too. It's just wise to make sure this person is also able to add their opinions.

You will need:

A large flipboard with paper / a large dry erase board
Markers / dry erase markers
Uninterrupted time and space
A person to guide the practice below
A person to take notes (more than one if it is a group with more than 10 people)

Schedule a time for the entire group to come together. I would encourage you to begin with creating sacred space (casting a circle, calling in elements and allies, invoking Hestia) so that you have a strong container for this important work. Once this is settled, I encourage you to have each person check-in about how they are feeling and what they might need to share to feel fully present.

After this feels complete, I suggest a practice like this:

If you like, you can close your eyes or soften your gaze, thinking about anything that might be pulling at your attention. Allow those distractions to settle and drop to the ground or wind themselves back up to you instead of away from you. You can also choose to cut these energetic distractions, so you feel free and wholly present.

Once this feels complete, I invite you to settle your awareness into the place of your heart. Allow your awareness to be present, noticing the speed of your heartbeat and the movement of your lungs. There is no need to change anything, just notice what is happening.

Allow that awareness and grounded feeling to drop to the place below your belly button, or the place of your will. See what it's like to have your grounded awareness there. How does it feel? What does it offer? What shifts as you do this?

On a breath, start to expand your awareness out beyond your body, beyond the room, and beyond the building you are in. Let this expanded awareness open to possibilities and ideas.

In this space, the guide can offer questions like, 'What does this wider awareness have to say about our community's values and vision?'

This question can be repeated, as needed. The participants are invited to share anything that arrives for them in this experience. These might be words, images, or other phrases of interest. The notetaker(s) will write down as much as they can grasp, allowing the information to be captured on paper or the dry erase board.

You can continue this practice for as long as it is generative. When things feel they are getting quieter, the guide can ask if there are any other things to say or share. If things continue to be quiet and it seems people are complete, then you can close out the practice in this way.

With gratitude to Hestia and our allies, we can begin to pull our awareness back into our bodies, allowing it to take up the space of our abdomen and will without being expanded beyond our skin. See what feels right for you and what you might need to become present in the room again. You might slowly move your body and open your eyes. You might drink some water or get a snack. You might look around the room to connect with others.

When you don't have a guide or a notetaker that is separate from the group, remember to include their shares in the process. They can also contribute and add to the process. If this is challenging for them, it is wise to do this practice again with them as part of a new sharing from their expanded awareness.

I personally have done this practice while being a facilitator and a notetaker, so it is possible, but if the practice is new, it's ideal to have a separate process to ensure you are able to completely immerse in the wisdom of a wider awareness.

At this point, you might decide that is enough to do for your group in the moment, open sacred space, and be done, or you can continue to the next section's practices. It's up to you. But I would strongly recommend this first practice before others since it helps to have something generative to start.

Creating Purpose & Mission

Once you have a sense of things people are bringing into the room, you can use the information to inform what happens next. If you're starting again, I encourage you to begin with sacred space to establish the container. If you are continuing, you can re-energize the space with an offering to Hestia.

A purpose will help you better understand the goal of your community. This allows you to have a sort of compass for whatever you choose to do together. Whenever things get murky or challenging, you will have something to look at to remind you of what's important to everyone. This can often get things back on track more than any other process. Reminders of why you're here allow you to reconnect with something bigger than a momentary hiccup in community.

Using the writings that you captured in the previous exercise; it can help to have a process in place to make decisions as a group. I have used consensus-based decision-making as part of being in the Reclaiming tradition of witchcraft, and it is a practice used in other activist groups.

A brief outline looks like this:

You meet as a group to make decisions about certain items. These items go onto an agenda. Each item can have its own time block and order of importance. Items should be things the group has information and opinions on so decisions can be made.

There are roles in the meeting: facilitator, notetaker, timekeeper, and vibes watcher.

- The facilitator leads the meeting, making sure everyone gets a chance to speak and keeping the conversation moving and within shared agreements.
- The notetaker takes notes of the meeting, not every word, but the things that will help keep a record of how the decision was made.

- The timekeeper watches the time and lets the group know when certain times for discussion are done or almost done.

- The vibes watcher is someone who can watch the group and point out when people's energy seems off or in need of attention.

Basic rules for engagement an include these:

- People speak one at a time, raising their hand to indicate they want to talk next.
  - A facilitator might interrupt to keep people from straying from the current agenda point.
  - A notetaker might interrupt if they need clarification on a note or need something repeated.
  - A timekeeper might interrupt to make sure people are aware of the time.
  - A vibes watcher might interrupt to point out an energy shift.
- Everyone is invited to share their opinions, and people should monitor their speaking time to ensure everyone has a chance to share.
- Conversations use 'I' statements as each person speaks to their own experience.
- There is an agreed upon time container for the whole meeting and each agenda item. If there is a need for more time, the whole group needs to agree to that.
- The goal is to discuss an item and then create a proposal for agreement. This proposal needs to be consensed on by the entire group to be complete. If someone does not agree with the proposal, they might offer an alternative. Then the group checks for consensus. If agreed to, then it is complete. Repeat as needed.

- The group is more important than the individual. This is a process in which all voices are valued, but not everyone will get what they want every time. The goal of consensus is to identify what can be agreed to since it serves most.
- Everyone agrees to listen and not to repeat what someone else has said.
- The ideas are everyone's ideas once they are shared, e.g., it is not "Irisanya's idea," is the idea of the group.

The group moves through agenda items until done or until the time container is complete. If things are not attended to in the meeting, they can move to the next meeting or an agreement to contract for more time can be made.

In creating the purpose and the mission, this meeting could look like this:

- Choose roles.
- Do a personal check-in to see how people are feeling.
- Reread the notes from the visioning practice.
- Each person shares what they feel is coming through for a purpose and mission.
- The facilitator summarizes what they have heard, asks for confirmation from the group, and adjusts the summary based on feedback.
- The facilitator asks for a proposal that outlines the purpose and mission of the group.
- One idea is heard at a time, ideally, but if there are more, there can be multiple proposals at the same time.
- The facilitator repeats each proposal and asks if there is agreement or if friendly amendments are needed.
- This continues until a proposal is consensed on for the group.
- Celebration!

One of the things I appreciate about this process is how in alignment with Hestia it is. This is a process in which everyone has a say, and all are working to support the larger good. In doing so, it is possible to have a peaceful conversation that is rooted in what is important versus what one person might want.

What I also appreciate about consensus is that it takes the time to listen to everyone so that everyone is agreeing to something wholeheartedly. You are not coming to a decision that people sort of appreciate, as you have listened to concerns along the way. While true there are more steps to this process in terms of challenging decision-making, I have given you the bare bones of what will likely work at this point of community building. I will also include resources at the end of this book for more in depth consensus information.

Of course, there are times when this process is going to have troubles. The most common places of trouble are:

- Straying from the agenda topic.
- Not listening to others and repeating something already said.
- Getting too attached to an idea.
- Focusing on one person's idea.
- Not following the agreements for conduct.
- Proposing an agenda item without enough information.
- Talking about agenda items that don't need a decision.

My best advice in this process is always to follow the agreements and come back to those, and the rest of the practice will take care of itself.

In time and likely in a meeting or two, you will find a purpose and mission for your group. This will help you better understand what you want to do and how you will do it. With this work of deciding on your mission together, you will be able to build a hearth that sustains itself.

Building a Hearth

We have talked about physical and non-physical hearths, but now I want to talk about a community hearth. Based on what you have already discussed and agreed to, this is likely to become clearer for your group. You will notice there is one (or more) missions the group is energized by. This is a good thing! The more energy you have behind something, the more energy you will have to give in the days ahead.

So, what do you want to do together? What do you want to create and build for others to gather around? Do you want to gather with a larger community, or do you want to create something that's just around a group of friends?

Here are some ideas for a hearth that celebrates Hestia:

- **Create agreements** – The best start is to have agreements that your group will follow. This way, you not only have a foundation, but you also have a place to go back to when things don't feel like they're working. In addition, agreements serve to build trust. The more the group follows the agreements, the more trust you create amongst each other. You know you will show up as you have promised to show up.
- **Meet regularly** – It's best to have a group that meets regularly so you can foster rapport and trust. Not every meeting needs to be productive or lead to an important decision, but regular meetings help to create a sustainable flow of energy. You can try to meet monthly at first and then see if more or fewer meetings would help.
- **Give feedback** – Trust is also borne out of being willing to share what is and isn't working. Notice I included 'what is working,' since it's common to think of feedback only as something that seeks to correct a problem. Spend

time each meeting talking about what is working in the group and what could work better. This attention will help to attend to issues when they arrive and are easier to manage.

- **Update agreements and vision** – On a regular basis, it is wise to look at the agreements and vision to make sure they still serve the group. People change and your group is likely to change too.
- **Decide on membership** – It can help for the original group to decide who gets to join and how they join. What does it mean to be a member of the group? What is expected? How long does one stay? How does one leave?
- **Create a conflict resolution process** – The best way to be ready for conflict is to decide how you will handle it before it happens. A process that I've seen work well is this:
  - The people in conflict talk to each other first to see if they can resolve what is happening between them. This should be done as soon as possible after the initial hurt.
  - If the people cannot resolve the conflict amongst themselves, then the conflict is brought to the group. The group hears from those in conflict, offers suggestions for resolution. The people in conflict agree or not to the suggestions.
  - If the group cannot help the people in conflict, a third party is brought in to help mediate the conflict. This can be done with each person in the conflict also bringing a support person with them to witness the mediation. The people in the mediation agree to a resolution or not.
  - If the mediation does not work, a person or persons in the group may be asked to leave or may choose to leave.

- **Have fun together** – One of the best ways to prevent burnout is to have fun together too. It's not just about meetings and decisions; you also want to have meals together, go do things together, and know each other as real people.

I have been a part of a few hearth groups, all of which lasted if the group was happy about the way things were held. Over time, people grew apart and priorities changed. But from each of these groups, it was clear these hearths were just what was needed to serve a purpose. And what I learned from each group is what I am passing onto you now.

Community Care

There is a quote that travels around the internet via a meme that sounds like this, "Sometimes we focus on self-care as the answer in a situation where community care is the answer." (To me, I think of Hestia saying this to the world as a whole.) It is common in the world today to focus on the idea of caring for one's self instead of thinking about interdependence and mutual aid.

In modern Western society, capitalism thrives off people who think they need to buy things to be better or happy, or both. To keep money flowing, advertising and other messaging seeks to make sure people are sold the idea that they must take care of their problems on their own. But is this really the case? Is this how humans are hardwired for survival? If you're shaking your head no, you're right.

Groups of humans have lived in communities for all time. They lived with their families and other peoples to have support to survive in harsh conditions. It was ideal to have people in a group who would handle certain tasks to support others doing other tasks. This cooperative model led to free time for creation and innovation, and eventually this produced art, music, and poetry, as well as innovations in movement and production.

While there is much more to this story than I will include, here's what I think is important about this progression: people made money from innovations and people wanted to make more money. Over time, people were told to 'succeed,' they had to have their own house, their own items, and their own space. This separated people from groups and caused a focus on rugged individualism in the United States, for example.

Though this may have seemed like a progressive way to live and a natural improvement, it has also caused society to move away from the idea of community care. People didn't gather at a communal hearth anymore; they wanted to buy their own and only share it with certain people.

I don't know about you, but I know I sometimes have more to do than I think I can handle. I wish I had my family nearby and that I had a group of people to help me when things are tough. While this used to be the standard in the past, community care is now something that needs to be brought back – a community care revolution is vital to keep ourselves well cared for and to make communities sustainable.

We genuinely cannot do everything we are 'supposed' to do on our own. To refer back to the idea of sharing our resources where we can, here are some more ideas to bring community care back to your group and to the hearth you create.

- Childcare support.
- Errands and other life tasks.
- Asking how another's day is and listening.
- Building relationships with neighbors and locals.
- Attending local political meetings.
- Voting and helping people get to voting polls.
- Creating support groups to listen to each other.

- Designing a needs and resources board for your local community, where you can list what you need and offer what you can give on a spreadsheet or website.

Sustainability is not just the practice of not spending all your time and money on a cause. It is also helping to create space for others to not spend all their time or resources on just what they need to do to live. And this community care begins with being able to ask for help from someone else. It begins with being praised for asking for help instead of being judged.

Some ideas for boosting community care include:

- Creating a social media group where people can ask for help.
- Setting up a prayer or candle altar where people can share their needs.
- Tracking when families need help with a new child or a death in the family.
- Developing and sharing a contact list of people who can help with certain tasks, e.g., if you need help with organizing, contact John Doe at this number, etc.
- Have regular community meetings that ask what people need.

This is not a perfect process, of course. And there will be times when a need can't be met because not everyone is able to help all the time. But your group might be willing to get things started by asking who wants to help. In doing so, this will energize people to participate and as more people get help, more people can help in the ways they can.

Rituals for Community

With the support of Hestia, you can strengthen your community, however you define this and whatever your goals might be. To help you, I am offering some basic templates for rituals you can do for certain community situations. In time, you will create rituals you need for the unique needs of your group, and for those who want to have a starting point, here are some offerings.

Ritual: Coming Together

This ritual works well for the start of your group and to solidify the energy of coming together.

Create sacred space – indigenous acknowledgement, ground, circle casting, allies, etc.

Call to Hestia – use an invocation that celebrates Her and invites Her to join you.

- Standing in a circle, have each person say their name and what they bring to this group. Have other circle members repeat the person's name three times and welcome them to the group. Repeat until everyone has had a chance to speak.
- Invite everyone to close their eyes or soften their gaze, thinking about what the group is going to do together. Let this be a gentle, free-flowing sharing of ideas and images that come to mind. If one person starts an idea, another person might continue it. Or a new idea might be shared and that one gets added to. The goal of this is to work together to create a word soup of ideas and excitement.
- Once the ideas start to subside, open your eyes, and look around at each other. You might share how excited you feel and how you are committed to working together for these visions or those that arrive in the future. Come together in a circle, getting closer and closer (if this feels right), and take a breath together. Take another breath together. And another.
- Once you are breathing together, one person can start a wordless tone (a hum or a one-note sound), and everyone

can join in. Continue to tone together until it naturally falls away. Feel the energy that arrives in the natural collaboration that you have at this moment.

- Allow things to be quiet for a few moments, listening with your ears and heart for any wisdom from Hestia. Once things feel settled, you can thank Hestia, thank allies and elements, and open the circle.
- Share food together, offering the first bite to Hestia.

Ritual: Cultivating Belonging & Togetherness

To continue to foster belonging and togetherness, you can use this ritual with the current group or when inviting new people into the group.

Create sacred space – indigenous acknowledgement, ground, circle casting, allies, etc.

Call to Hestia – offer an invocation that speaks of belonging and community

In this ritual space, I encourage an ally circle practice. This is a practice I learned in Reclaiming, but it originates from activist spaces and likely from indigenous practices.

It helps to have a person who is 'leading' this and talking folks through the process.

Stand in a circle. Step in one at a time and say something that is true for the person stepping in, e.g., I know I belong when _____. Keep the statement simple and short. There is no need to explain or justify what is said.

Those who resonate will step into the middle with the first person. Everyone in the center will make eye contact with those who step into the circle too. The leader might say something like, *Notice who stands with you and shares this experience.*

After an inner circle connection is made, the leader says, *Turn out to see all who support you.* Go glow. Let it stop a second before *And step back into the circle.*

If no one steps in the center with someone, the leader can say something like: *Notice how you stand in the center of so many people that support you, even if they don't share the same experience. You are not alone.*

Let everyone have a chance to go once before stepping in a second time. If things start to slow down, the leader can ask if there are any more that want to step in. When it's done, have people look around and thank each other who shared and stood in witness and support. If someone doesn't want to or cannot step in, they can say their name in the center with what they want to say or support someone else.

This process can go on for as long as it feels helpful and supportive to the participants. You might notice that people will change to other topics as this is an organic process of intimacy-building. Because it is this, there are ways that you cannot control what people want to have witnessed.

It is important to be clear that all ideas are welcome, that all people belong. If there are times when a statement is challenging or it is traumatic, which does happen, it is wise to have the guide or another person in the group remind everyone to breathe. Move slowly in this practice and allow it to be gentle. There is no need to rush.

Once it is done, you can come together in a shared hug or eye contact with everyone. Then you can devoke Hestia and other allies (releasing them from the circle with gratitude), open the circle, and feast together.

Ritual: Navigating Conflict

It is Hestia's glory that, alone of the great Olympians, she never takes part in wars or disputes (Graves 74).

While the beginning of any group can feel so hopeful that conflict is the last thing you consider, it is wise to prepare for this ahead of time. With the watchful eyes of the kind and graceful Hestia, you will be able to navigate conflict with a process, but also a ritual.

Ideally, this ritual should be in a place that is comfortable for all who are attending. It should include the people in conflict whenever possible, but if not, then this ritual will work to hold the conflict as an entity.

As with any ritual, create sacred space. For this ritual, it is wise to create a strong container to hold what needs to be held. Invoke Hestia as the wise one, the hearth that doesn't go out, and the one who holds community in all its phases.

Take a bowl and place it at the center of the circle. Into this bowl, you can each write something about the conflict. You might choose to read what you have written, e.g., the feelings you have, the things you have learned, any questions you have, etc. This is a time to remain honest and curious about the conflict. It is not a time to be judgmental or to try to solve anything.

This bowl can then be passed around the circle for everyone to see. Each person can take a piece of paper out of the bowl and sit it beside them. When everyone has a piece of paper, one person at a time can read what is on the paper, take a breath and respond in a loving and curious way.

Here are some examples:

- **I am sad** → I feel the sadness of this person. I honor the sadness of this person.
- **I have learned about my stubbornness and defensiveness** → I see this person in learning about themselves and I honor their ongoing commitment to being willing to see themselves fully.
- **I wonder what the best way forward is** → I hear the desire to resolve the situation and honor the possibility that the way forward will present itself at the right time.

The point of the 'answers' is not to solve anything or even to end the conflict. The point of this ritual is to create space for feelings and learnings to be witnessed and honored. In my experience, just stating that someone's feelings are valid is enough to move ahead to a grounded place where people can work things out without blame or malice.

Once people have had a chance to witness and be witnessed, it can help to lay on the floor or ground together, heads in the middle. In that place, share feelings that you have and how they are impacting you at this moment. You might share what has shifted or what you have learned from this ritual. Together, you might ask Hestia to bless what happens next.

As things settle down, you might hum or tone together until things feel complete.

Thank Hestia and the allies. Open the circle and just be with each other instead of trying to problem solve. Leave problem solving for another day.

Ritual: Transitions

For this ritual, you will need to adapt things based on the type of transition. I will try to give many different options to ensure you have enough ideas to figure out what works best for your needs.

As with any ritual, I encourage you to create sacred space to maintain a container of safety and steadiness. Depending on the transition, you might need different things or decide to use other materials than what I suggest.

I think everyone in this ritual should bring a candle that represents them. This can be lit during the invocation to Hestia, as everyone is a part of that flame.

If this is a ritual of bringing in a new member, then this person can be brought into the center, introduce themselves and their talents. Everyone can witness and celebrate them and then each person can hold a candle and send energy to their journey.

The new member can light their candle, adding themselves to the hearth. Celebrate!

If this is a ritual of a member leaving, then the person can come into the center with their candle, sharing what they have learned and how they have grown or gained insights. Each member can then hold that candle, passing it around while sharing what they have gained from this person. Then when this is done, the person who is leaving can hold their candle, saying anything else they need to say, and blow their candle out. Celebrate this transition!

If this is a ritual of shifting agreements, you might choose to burn the old agreements and send energy into the new agreements by holding the paper they might be written on. You can thank the old and say the new agreements into the sacred space for Hestia to bless.

No matter what you have done, it helps to connect in the end with song, physical touch, sharing water or food, etc. Once the ritual seems complete, thank Hestia and other beings before opening the circle.

Trance: Traveling to the Heart of Community

A practice I have been taught and still teach is the practice of group trance. This is a trance working that brings people together to travel in the liminal spaces and to guide each other in the energy that arrives. In this book, we have already started to work in these ways, but this practice will be one you can use when you are working together in a more solidified group. In my experience, group trance works best with three or more people, so this is something to keep in mind.

What you will need:

A group of three or more

A person who is willing to lead a grounding practice (labeled below)
Willingness to participate with spoken words

Ideally, you would gather in a space that is large enough for everyone to lay down with their heads near each other, forming a circle. You can also choose to lay on the ground beside each other in other patterns, or you can choose to have some people sit if that's helpful for their bodies. The main goal is to be comfortable and to be in places where you can hear each other speak.

A grounding practice you can use is this:

I invite you to find a way for your body to be comfortable and to be connected with others in the room. You should be able to hear what others are saying and they should be able to hear what you might say aloud. Take some time to settle your body and begin to breathe in a way that feels supportive and soothing. You might choose to extend your breath or just simply notice it. You might choose to notice your heartbeat, or you might choose to tense and relax your muscles to bring yourself into your body, knowing you are safe and sound.

As the group continues to relax, allow any tension or worry or expectation to drop into the floor or ground beneath you. Imagine the earth taking this extra energy and composting it into something that is helpful and nourishing. Take the time you need, and when you are feeling settled, you might say something like, "I am ready for this journey." We'll wait until everyone is ready before we begin the next steps.

Now that everyone is ready, we are going to go on a journey to meet with Hestia. We are going to follow Her to the hearth to see what she has to offer for our community. Can one person start us off in the direction of Her hearth? You might say that you see all of us walking on a path made of well-worn dirt, etc. Once this journey begins, we will each take turns moving us toward Hestia and to the hearth to receive any wisdom.

We will also trust that when it is time to return that someone will bring us back this way to come back to this room.

Group trance is not something that is scripted out, so there is a lot of mystery in what might happen next and what might be possible in this trance. You can do this trance again and again and still get new insights and images.

The goal is to have everyone participate in some way. If things feel too quiet, you might ask a question like, 'And what happens now?' to get things started again. Or you might let things be silent until someone naturally finds the words to talk about what happens next. It's crucial that everyone listen so they can add to what is already flowing versus creating something dissonant.

However, if people are called to say something that is very odd because they have a strong feeling about something, they can also say it. After all, sometimes the things that seem the most out of place may be the things people need to hear.

Group trance is also a great exercise for cultivating group think. You might do group trance together regularly enough that you can visualize or feel the hearth you have encountered. Many groups will have maps in their minds for places they can go together. When this is possible, your group might also be able to be in separate places and travel to Hestia, the hearth, together.

Chapter 8

Cultivating a Modern Relationship with Hestia

Aristonoos' Hymn to Hestia, third quarter 4th c. BCE

Holy Queen of Sanctity,
we hymn you, Hestia, whose abiding realm
is Olympus and the middle point of earth
and the Delphic laurel tree!
You dance around Apollo's towering temple
rejoicing both in the tripod's mantic voices
and when Apollo sounds the seven strings
of his golden phorminx and, with you,
sings the praises of the feasting gods.
We salute you, daughter of Kronos
and Rhea, who alone brings firelight
to the sacred altars of the gods;
Hestia, reward our prayer, grant
wealth obtained in honesty: then we shall always
dance around your glistening throne.
Greek Hymns: Volume I by William D. Furley and
Jan Maarten Bremer

For many, the idea of working with Hestia may be new. After all, Hestia's siblings and other Greek godds are much more present in the modern world. There aren't a lot of folks I know who are devoted to Hestia or even to Vesta. While there are many who I know to be committed to community-building and growing, they do not seem to ground this in a deity as far as I know.

If you are called to working with Hestia, I encourage you to follow a practice of intentional relationship-building. This will help you create a solid foundation for ongoing work, especially if you are also building or supporting a community in your life (or want to be). Like any relationship, relationships take time, effort, and intention. They are not built with one altar or one prayer; relationships with deities require progressive interactions and commitment.

While you don't have to commit to being with a deity forever (I promise), any relationship building should include some basic steps.

Meeting & Greeting

A good way to start building a relationship with any deity is to learn more about them. You might begin with an internet search or by reading a book. In this way, you can start to see what is being said about this godd and whether it's something that is of interest to you. Just like doing a background check on a person you might date, this initial research might yield answers or information that doesn't sit right with you. And if so, then you can stop what you're doing and move onto another godd. (My hope is that by this part of the book, it's probably clear that Hestia is someone you want to get to know better.)

I personally start working with deities by following this process:

Research

Whenever I get a hunch about working with deities, I want to learn more, especially if I don't already have an idea about their background, energies, or myths. I will do what you're doing: read about them. I will go to different websites to see what others have said. I will also go to places where I feel their energy might reside. For example, when I started working with Artemis, I would go to the forest a lot because I felt her there.

I have also started to read about the cultures in which deities were worshiped or honored. This tells me a bit more about how to interpret the stories about them. After all, what makes sense to me in my modern world may not make as much sense in the ancient world.

In addition, I might reach out to friends who have worked with these deities in the past. They can sometimes offer me insights based on their personal experience, as well as offer me resources I haven't found yet.

Reflection

Once I have this information, I focus on seeing how that feels in my body. More often than not, I will work with a deity based on a feeling I had. But I might also work with a deity because I have to work with them for a Witchcamp, class, or ritual. In those cases, I will try to move away from my head and into my heart so I can drop into the magick of the being.

My reflection phase can consist of journaling about the deity, what I think of them, and how they might be showing up in my life. I might set up an altar and have a picture or statue of them. I might start to sit at the altar to see if I have any experiences or if I have any new information shared with me in this practice.

Some find that closing their eyes and thinking about Hestia can help them connect. Think about what She might look like, based on what we know, and think about how She might show up if someone were asking for Her help or attention. You might want to create art for Her or you might decide you want to sing or cook for Her in these moments.

This part of relationship-building can be likened to dating and getting to know someone. When you aren't with them, you are thinking about them and thinking about what they might have to offer to you. You are considering if you like them and what you might not like. And yes, even the godds can have red flags[22] that don't work for you.

Attention

While this might seem like a step-by-step process, it doesn't have to be. You can continue to learn and reflect throughout a relationship. It is also advisable to consider how much attention you can give in your relationship with Hestia. Unlike other godds, She doesn't seem to need a lot of attention, but in the beginning, I think any deity is looking to see if their dedicant or devotee is willing to prioritize the relationship.

Building an altar space for Her is ideal. This can be a small altar on a shelf or desk, or it could be something larger. (There are more ideas later in the book when your relationship gets more involved or committed.) The godds like to have a place where their energy is focused and settled. When they have this space, they recognize what you think of them, even when you're not in the same room.

Of course, this doesn't have to mean hours of time with a deity, but it also could mean that in some relationships. You might want and the godd might need more time together to figure out if you're a good fit. I encourage you to dedicate some time each day to get to know a new deity. You can take just five minutes every morning to sit at their altar or to sit with your thoughts focused on them. This will help you see how the relationship feels and how it works for the both of you.

You might also decide you want to have longer 'dates' with your deity. Some like to spend hours on weekends with their godds or decide certain phases of the moon to their deities. You get to decide what works best for you, and because you have done some research, you may already have a sense of what might work for Hestia. I personally think working with Her before a meal or in meal preparation is a great connecting point.

I also think giving a small offering to Hestia before every meal is a way to give Her more attention.

Trusting Your Intuition & Messages

Throughout your relationship building with Hestia, it is wise to journal about what you have noticed in your life. What has changed? What has improved? What is more important? What has become less important? What messages have you heard from Her? What messages have you seen from Her in the world around you?

Documenting these things in some way will help you see just how far your relationship has progressed. It also helps to be reminded of things that sparked interest for you or that ended up being direct messages you needed to hear. I know I can't remember the details of the everyday, but I enjoy looking back on things to remind myself of the magick.

Again, it is wise to check in with your body to see what the relationship feels like.

- Does it feel safe?
- Does it feel comfortable?
- Is there trust or the willingness to trust?
- Do you feel nourished?
- Do you feel exhausted?

If some of these questions start to sound like questions you could ask in any relationship, you're right. In any relationship, it is wise to consider whether things feel right and good to you. You should check in about this with yourself in the beginning so you can sense if things aren't quite right or if things aren't working out the way you wanted them to. 'It's not them, it's you' happens in relationships with deities too.

If you don't feel things are working out, you can just step back from any other interactions. You don't have to keep working with a deity, even if it seemed natural at first. You don't have to keep working with a godd because it sounds like the right thing to do. You can say no. You can step away. You are in charge of and responsible for your decisions.

NOTE: One thing I often see in folks who are building relationships with deities is that they don't know what to do when they feel weird about a certain godd. There might be no other description or reason for this weirdness, but when you feel weird or like you shouldn't be working with a deity, you should stop. It doesn't matter if it's unclear or if nothing has 'gone wrong.' I would encourage you to just stop.

Side story from me: there is a deity who I don't work with in public settings anymore because every time I did, someone in my family would get very sick. I don't know if it was just a coincidence, but it happened often enough that I have made a personal promise to not work with them in public anymore. I still have a statue of them, and I have still read their stories, but something about them doesn't feel right, so I don't do more.

The first stages of working with a deity can take as long as they take. You don't have to make quick decisions and you don't have to commit to being a devotee for the rest of your life. You can take your time in getting to know them and getting to know yourself in this relationship too.

Expectations & Agreements

Like any good relationship, you want to move into a conversation about what you want it to look like. What do you really want? What are you prepared to offer? What do you think about the level of commitment? Often at this point, I see people talk about waiting to see what the godd wants to offer them, which is understandable when so many people move from a religion or practice in which deities are seen as being all-knowing and all-powerful.

While I don't disagree that the godds have a wider range of experience and perspective, often offering wisdom that I don't have yet, I do not consider deities to be better or greater than me. I see deity relationships as non-hierarchical as I want them to be reciprocal in nature. My work with the godds is based on asking for what I want and need, and listening to what a godd wants and needs from me. In doing so, we can build lasting trust for a long-term relationship.

If this is what you want too, I suggest starting with a list of what you want from the relationship with Hestia. How might you define it? What do you call it? What do you expect from Her and what can you do in return? This process might take some time to complete, and it is certainly a list of things that require examination and review over time. After all, your needs might change. The godd's needs might change.

You can do this as a piece of paper with the expectations and agreements clearly listed. This way, you can return to this piece of paper for review and editing. I don't have a piece of paper anymore, but I do return to deities to review our relationship to see if it's still working.

(As you might have noticed by now, I think it wise to approach relationships with deities as you would approach relationships with humans.)

It's kind to yourself and to the deity to be as honest and clear as you can. You want to know if this is something that will work out for you, or not. And in writing this list out, you could uncover your own limitations. After all, you might realize Hestia wants to cook with you, but you don't like to cook. You might decide you don't want to do that and that other acts of service are also not things you want to do. These are just examples, but I hope they start to show why this sort of starting point is important.

Too often, I see people working with deity as though the godd is a gumball machine. Some feel they can just insert a few coins of attention or offerings and expect to get a prize. This is not only disrespectful of the deity, but it is also a poor way to be in relationships. Instead, I offer the model of giving and taking, offering, and receiving. I also offer the idea that the relationship is not something that is assured just because you do a ritual one time. Just like any relationship, working with Hestia requires ongoing commitment and action.

Here are other questions to consider in your agreements:

- What time can I set aside for this relationship?
- What resources do I have (or not)?
- How do I expect to feel in this relationship?
- What do I not want to do?
- What do I want to do?
- How will I know things are working? How will I know when things aren't working?
- What are my limits?

You don't have to answer these questions, but you will want to think about what the relationship will look and feel like when you are both doing what you promised to do. And even then, if things don't end up working out, you can know you tried your very best.

Navigating the Everyday

Just like any relationship, things can get boring over time. You can't have the excitement of 'new relationship energy' with your godds every day. It's not realistic and it's just not workable for anyone involved. But what you can do is start to think about what everyday practices might look like for your partnership.

My experience is that different godds need different levels of attention to feel special and honored. So you may need to try a few things to see what works best. Here are some ideas for navigating the everyday with Hestia.

Daily Practices

Hestia is a godd I would define as being a bit more every day. To me, this means She is ingrained in everything that happens, so it's not so much about being dramatically devotional with Her as much as it is maintaining awareness. After all, when She is everywhere, it can be easy to forget why you're doing the things you're doing.

- Morning meeting – Greeting the godds in the morning is a wise practice, especially for Hestia. Greet Her at an altar or another special space. Thank Her for Her ongoing blessings and invite Her to support you in the day as you light a candle that can safely stay lit.
- Mealtime offerings – It makes sense to give small offerings to Hestia before each meal you cook or eat. This means you want to do this even outside of your house or when you're at restaurants. You don't have to make a scene of it, rather you can just take a small portion of the food and place it on the side of a plate in honor of Her.
- Nighttime tending – Before bed, I suggest you think about how to 'turn off' the hearth of Hestia for the night. This can include going to the places where you might have light and thanking Her for these spaces. You could also take time to put out a candle you lit in the morning as an even more focused practice of greeting and farewell.
- Blessings or prayers – I find saying things aloud or in my head to Hestia is a helpful practice of attention. You can choose to use something that you have written, or you can be spontaneous. This helps to bring any wandering attention back to Her.

These daily practices need not be hours long to be effective or respectful. In fact, the easier you make a daily practice, the more likely you are to keep it up. And please know right now that there will be days when you forget or rush; it's okay. Even the godds understand that you're not going to be perfect all the time. This is why it's called a 'practice.'

Hearth Rituals

After reading the hearth section, I imagine you already have ideas about how to use the hearth to continue to build your relationship with Hestia. Finding ways to bring your attention back to flame or fire is the goal of these rituals.

- **Daily reverence** – You can use some of the daily practices in the place where you consider Hestia and Her hearth to be. This can be as simple as lighting a candle or as complex as cleaning the hearth every day to make sure it is fit for Her presence.
- **Monthly renewal** – I would also recommend some hearth maintenance, and not just someone who comes out to check your fireplace. It's wise to go back to the space of your hearth each month to see if it needs something new from you or if Hestia has suggested any new practices for Her. Perhaps on the first or the last day of the month, you can check in with the hearth to see what it might need for ongoing power.
- **Annual ritual** – I like the idea of having a larger cleaning, lighting, and blessing ritual each year for Hestia. You can do this more often, of course, but since Hestia does seem to want things to be sustainable, an annual ritual would be perfect.

Coming back to the hearth again and again is the same action as coming back to Hestia. You will want to do this regularly so the power of this place and magick continues to grow and hold the home.

Gratitude Workings

Hestia offers so much to the daily lives of people that giving thanks is an honorable practice. While any of the practices have an element of gratitude in them, here are some other suggestions to continue this work.

- **Journal of gratitude** – You can create a journal into which you can list all of the things you're grateful for in your family and home life. This can be a journal you decorate for Hestia, or it can be plain and simple, just as She is usually described. Over the time you come back to restore your hearth, you can read from this journal to remember the blessings you have enjoyed.
- **Papers of thanks** – A common practice is to write down things you are grateful for and give them to the godds in a bowl on an altar. Those slips of paper can stay in the bowl or other special container for as long as you like. You might choose to burn them when they are overflowing, reading them before you burn each one. Others might like to write down their pieces of gratitude on a slip of paper, read it to Hestia, and then burn it immediately, watching the smoke go up to Her on Mount Olympus.
- **Ongoing gratefulness** – It can also be as simple as saying what you're grateful for as you are noticing things in your life. You can start to say aloud or in your mind, 'Thank you Hestia.' This simple practice will return your awareness to the connection of your relationship and what it offers to you in many moments.

Being grateful allows your relationship with Hestia to grow, and it helps your mind focus on what is working well in your life. Though there will be times when things are rough, and this is normal and expected, there are often always things for which to be grateful. And the more you can turn to recognizing that, the more you will find.

Working with other Godds

Something that isn't discussed at length, from what I've seen, is what to do when you are working with other godds besides Hestia. What do you do when you already have godds in your daily practices and rituals? First, I think it's wise to consider what each godd already wants from you. In thinking about this, you can more thoughtfully consider whether you have the space for another deity relationship. If you decide you are ready to have another godd in the mix of your practice, here are some other questions to consider:

- How do these godds get along in mythology?
- Are these godds familiar with each other?
- What are the energies? Do they complement each other?

For example, do you think you want to work with Hestia and Her siblings? If so, what might come up as a result? Do the energies seem to fit what you want to invite into your life? If not, then maybe wait on adding new deity relationships to your Hestia partnership.

You may find you have other questions to ask of yourself and the godds before you make any final decisions. Of course, you can always start with one arrangement with the godds and then change the structures and agreements.

Here are some ways to work with multiple godds in kind and supportive ways:

- **Review any agreements you have in place** – It can help to review any agreements you already have in place with other deities. This way, you can be sure you are not over promising something you can't deliver to Hestia.

- **Schedule time for each godd** – I enjoy creating time blocks in my calendar for different godds, at least in the beginning of a relationship. This will help the godds all have the attention they want, but also within the parameters of your human schedule. In time, you may not need to set up such a stringent schedule, but at the start, it's better to be specific about what you are agreeing to.

- **Make space for each godd** – Each of the godds might need to have an altar space for themselves, so you need to consider this. You may want to have each godd on a different shelf or in a different room, depending on how you decide they get along. In my apartment, I have some godds in the same areas because they don't seem to mind sharing. But also, the main godds I work with get more than one altar, so I imagine that helps when they need to share space with other godds.

- **Be willing to adjust** – If this is a new practice to you, having more than one godd around, I advise you to be ready and willing to change things up if they don't feel right. You can have the best plan in place, and it might not feel right. You might add Hestia to an altar, only to notice your family time isn't as calm as it used to be. Try out new places and practices to see how things might shift.

- **Give things time** – Of course, not all practices and places need to be adjusted immediately when something feels off. Sometimes things not feeling right is not about the godds; it's just life. I encourage a bit of patience, maybe a week or two, before changing what you already have in place.

- **Pay attention** – In all of this is the assumption that you will be paying attention to what is happening in your deity's world and in your world. You might use a journal to track how things feel and what you decided to do to support each godd. This can provide a reference point if things seem to be moving in a not-so-great direction.

Overall, working with multiple godds can be done and it can be simple. It just takes a little navigation and awareness. In my experience, if you are tending to your godds well, you can easily have multiple deities in the same place. And if they don't get along, you can always move them apart, and that usually works to diffuse strange energy.

Troubleshooting Deity Relationships

Hestia is a low-drama deity, which can give the impression that She will be easy to work with: which is often true. But even so, I hear the same questions from folks who are working with deity, so I tend to include a little troubleshooting primer.

Here are some of the most common observations and complaints I hear:

- The deity is too quiet.
- The deity is too loud.
- I'm not getting what I want.
- I don't feel good about this relationship.
- I don't know what to do with the deity.

Here is the checklist I would review if I was facing any of these issues:

- Am I doing what I said I would do in my agreements?
- Am I showing up to listen or just to talk?
- What offerings have I made?
- How am I trying to learn more about the deity?
- Have I been consistent in my practices?

- What is the state of the altar? Does it need to be cleaned or tidied?
- Have I been honest about what I want from this deity?
- Have I shown any gratitude?
- Could I spend more time with this deity?

When you are not happy in a relationship with a human, the first thing you SHOULD do is sit down with them to talk about what is happening for you. You can do this with Hestia. You could create some sacred space, sit with Hestia, and listen to see what She might have to say to you. If you haven't been connecting with Her for that long, it might just be that you need to be patient and build a stronger relationship.

If it has been a longer period of time you have been in a relationship with Hestia, I find it helpful to think about my role in the relationship. How have I shown up? Could I do better? Have I been falling behind or becoming complacent?

Though it's common to want to blame the deity, I find it more productive to focus on what I have some control over: my actions and reactions. When I start to look at the things I have been doing (or likely have NOT been doing), I can see why things don't feel the way I want them to feel. I can then make some shifts and see what happens next.

What I think to be true is the fact that deities do want to have people to worship them. They do want people to remember their names and give them offerings. So when things aren't quite going the way you think they should be, turn back to your own actions to see if you're being a kind partner in the relationship or if you need to turn things around.

Dedicating to Hestia

When I dedicate myself to a deity, I am promising to sing their praises, often literally. I am committing to being in a relationship with them for a certain period of time or as long as it works for the both of us. You don't have to commit to anything for the rest of your life, and you can always step away from a relationship with a godd, if that seems like the right thing to do.

Feel free to adjust this ritual to suit your particular needs.

What you will need:

Candles (3), preferably in enclosed containers
Matches or a lighter
An image of Hestia
Piece of paper and writing utensil
Food and drink

You can also choose to create a large altar space for Hestia if that feels appropriate.

I would start with creating sacred space. Some like to cleanse the area with smoke from a local plant or the ring of a bell. You can then ground yourself into the space, so you are as present as possible. Cast a circle of protection and security.

Invite Hestia into your space by invoking Her with words, song, dance, etc. You can choose what feels best for your relationship and your level of commitment. If you're not sure what to say, I find Hestia (and other godds) like to hear their stories shared aloud. Or you could read any hymns with Hestia's name in them.

Once you feel that She is present, light the candles and place them in front of you on the ground or a table. Place the image of Hestia where you can see it and near the candles. In this space, I invite you to look at the flames for as long as you can. See how they move and what they might have to tell you in the way you glow. You can ask Hestia to show you what you need to see before you make any commitment.

As you feel these images and messages arrive, close your eyes. In this internal space, because to feel into what you need to promise to Hestia in this new dedication. You can be as detailed or as concise as you like, depending on the relationship you want to call in. Once you have sat with Her and felt into what you want from the relationship and what She wants from you, you can open your eyes and write this down.

Take your time to write down what you want. Once you are done, you can say these things aloud over the flames and to the image of Hestia. Notice how these agreements feel and if anything needs to be adjusted. If you feel settled, you can take a candle in your hand and look at the flame. Think about how Hestia is an eternal flame who can brighten and destroy.

Consider the flame you have inside of you right now. Ask that Hestia help you keep your fire growing and glowing.

Hestia, Eternal One, Eternal Flame,
I promise to serve you and to give you the first offering,
I honor your grace and your peaceful demeanor,
I commit to serving you to support the family of my heart
    and blood,

I dedicate myself to your wisdom and your resilience
I dedicate myself to you for a year and a day
To honor and keep your name alive in each breath.

Welcome Hestia to the hearth of my heart,
May our relationship be blessed and honorable.
Hail Hestia! Hail Flame and Hearth!
(Feel free to adjust this as needed.)

You can sit in this reverence for as long as you like. Sit to see if there are any more messages She wants to give to you or other agreements She wants you to take on. Take the food and drink, offering some to Her first before you have a small feast to end the celebration.

You can then thank Hestia for being there and close the circle.

Conclusion

> [Hestia] is also the last re-born because she contains the pattern of the transcendent macrocosm that we each as microcosm contain and beat (as in 'reproduce') in the second stage of life. The source contains and reflects all; beginnings are also endings. Hestia contains the central paradox of all human life. Thus she is, as Hesiod states, the chief of all Goddesses, not only because she is most venerated day-to-day, but because she is the source of all things (Demetrakopoulos 72-73).

Hestia is the beginning and the end, the one who was born and reborn. She is the source of life and sustenance and the one to watch over the family in all of its stages. If there is any godd that knows family, it's Hestia. She stands to the side, becoming the important and eternal flame, to keep the peace and to honor communities.

While Her stories are few, Her impact is wide and far-reaching. Hestia is a godd who seeks not only to connect, but also to ensure the ongoing connection. For me, She is the goddess who I turn to when I need help building or strengthening community. She reminds me it can be simple. She reminds me that humans are better when together, when working toward a sustainable community.

This is not an easy practice, and it will have times of disruption and disagreement. But with the energy of Hestia as a guide, communities can grow and thrive.

Sweet, calm Hestia,
You who are flame and hearth,
You who are everywhere and ongoing,

You who is the crackle of the fire,
And the whisper of wisdom,
Thank you for your blessings and your grace,
Thank you for the quiet presence
To remind us that community is a blessing
That coming together can be nourishing and sustainable

Hestia, we offer you the gifts of commitment and consistency,
We offer you the gift of our time and attention and integrity,
To do what we say we will do,
To provide what we said we would provide,
And to sit by the warmth the hearth
And remember even when flames die down, they can return.

Hestia, you of many homes and rooms,
May your blessings continue to inspire and transform,
May your guidance rise into our ears with the smoke of
    remembering our role in keeping these fires going.
Hail Hestia, Hail Hearth!

Endnotes

1. Prytaneion: town hall
2. https://mythopedia.com/topics/hestia
3. https://mythopedia.com/topics/hestia
4. https://www.britannica.com/topic/Hestia
5. https://www.greekmythology.com/Olympians/Hestia/hestia.html
6. https://www.ancient-origins.net/myths-legends-europe/hestia-0017291
7. https://en.wikipedia.org/wiki/Theatre_of_the_Oppressed
8. https://www.ancient-origins.net/myths-legends-europe/hestia-0017291
9. https://www.newworldencyclopedia.org/entry/Hestia#cite_ref-18
10. https://www.newworldencyclopedia.org/entry/Hestia#cite_ref-19
11. https://en.wikipedia.org/wiki/Amphidromia
12. https://www.worldhistory.org/Hestia/
13. https://www.worldhistory.org/Hestia/
14. https://chs.harvard.edu/chapter/1-defining-homeric-sacrifice/
15. https://hellenicfaith.com/do-ut-des/
16. https://www.greekmythology.com/Olympians/Hestia/hestia.html
17. https://en.wikipedia.org/wiki/Olympic_flame
18. https://en.wikipedia.org/wiki/Prometheus
19. https://journals.openedition.org/pallas/21157
20. https://fireecology.springeropen.com/articles/10.1007/BF03400631#:~:text=Naturally%20started%20wildfires%2C%20also%2C%20were,Homer%20in%20Iliad%20(%CE%9B.
21. https://en.wikipedia.org/wiki/Vitex_agnus-castus

22. Red flags are warning signs of danger; a phrase to describe a situation in which someone has a quality that is dangerous and/or not good for a relationship.

Additional Resources

Baring, Anne and Cashford, Jules. "The Myth of the Goddess: Evolution of an Image."

Connelly, Joan Breton. "Portrait of a Priestess: Women and Ritual in Ancient Greece."

Graziosi, Barbara. "The Gods of Olympus."

Henderson, Raechel. "The Scent of Lemon & Rosemary: Working Domestic Magick with Hestia."

Mankey, Jason and Astrea Taylor. "Modern Witchcraft with the Greek Gods: History, Insights & Magickal Practice."

Plaisance, Monte. "Hestia: Goddess of Peace, Home and Hearth."

Consensus Decision-Making Resources

https://thedecider.app/consensus-decision-making

https://www.betterevaluation.org/methods-approaches/methods/consensus-decision-making

https://pubs.opengroup.org/handbooks/consensus-decision-making/index.html

https://www.groupfacilitation.net/Articles%20for%20Facilitators/The%20Basics%20of%20Consensus%20Decision%20Making.pdf

https://www.tamarackcommunity.ca/hubfs/Resources/Tools/Practical%20Guide%20for%20Consensus-Based%20Decision%20Making.pdf

Bibliography

Burkert, Walter. "Greek Religion."

Demetrakopoulos, Stephanie A. "Hestia, Goddess of the Hearth."

Detienne, Marcel. "The Writing of Orpheus: Greek Myth in Cultural Context."

Evelyn-White, Hugh G., translation. "The Homeric Hymns and Homerica."

Goodrich, Norma Lorre. "Priestesses."

Graves, Robert. "The Greek Myths."

Hamilton, Edith. "Mythology,"

Hesiod. "Theogony and Works and Days," Translated by M.L. West.

Hitch, Sarah. "King of Sacrifice: Ritual and Royal Authority in the Iliad." https://chs.harvard.edu/chapter/1-defining-homeric-sacrifice/

Kerènyi, Karl. "Goddesses of Sun and Moon."

Lefkowitz, Mary R. "Women in Greek Myth." Second edition

Monaghan, Patricia. "The New Book of Goddesses & Heroines."

Paris, Ginette. "Pagan Meditations: The Worlds of Aphrodite, Artemis, and Hestia."

Pomeroy, Sarah B. "Goddesses, Whores, Wives, and Slaves."

Sedley, David. "The Etymologies in Plato's Cratylus." The Journal of Hellenic Studies.

Trzaskoma, Stephen M., Smith, R. Scott, and Brunet, Stephen, translators and editors. "Anthology of Classical Myth: Primary Sources in Translator," Second Edition.

Weigle, Marta. "Spiders & Spinsters: Women and Mythology"

http://greekreconmommy.blogspot.com/2011/07/old-essay-on-hestia-overlooked-olympian.html

https://doi.org/10.1007/BF03400631

https://paganreveries.wordpress.com/2012/05/02/hestia-the-queen-of-fire-part-one/

https://paganreveries.wordpress.com/2012/05/09/hestia-the-queen-of-fire-part-two/

https://hellenicfaith.com/do-ut-des/

https://www.theoi.com/Ouranios/Hestia.html

https://en.wikipedia.org/wiki/Titanomachy

https://www.theoi.com/Text/Apollodorus1.html

https://www.greekboston.com/culture/mythology/story-hestia/

https://en.wikipedia.org/wiki/Hestia

https://westportlibrary.libguides.com/hestia#:~:text=Hestia%20was%20the%20Greek%20virgin,daughter%20of%20Cronus%20and%20Rhea.

https://greekgodsandgoddesses.net/goddesses/hestia/

https://www.greekmythology.com/Olympians/Hestia/hestia.html

https://www.britannica.com/topic/Hestia

https://www.worldhistory.org/Hestia/

https://www.ancient-origins.net/myths-legends-europe/hestia-0017291

https://www.newworldencyclopedia.org/entry/Hestia

https://pantheon.org/articles/h/hestia.html

https://mythopedia.com/topics/hestia

https://www.perseus.tufts.edu/hopper/text?doc=Perseus%3Atext%3A1999.01.0138%3Ahymn%3D29

https://www.beautytherapyabsolution.com/en/learn/arts-culture/rendez-vous-divinites-hestia/#:~:text=An%20ancient%20ritual%2C%20called%20Amphidromia,the%20arms%20of%20his%20parents.

https://en.wikipedia.org/wiki/Amphidromia

https://otherworldlyoracle.com/hestia-goddess-of-the-hearth/

https://lunastationquarterly.com/hestia-the-enigma/

https://chs.harvard.edu/chapter/1-defining-homeric-sacrifice/

https://hellenicfaith.com/do-ut-des/

https://fireecology.springeropen.com/articles/10.1007/
    BF03400631#:~:text=Naturally%20started%20
    wildfires%2C%20also%2C%20were,Homer%20in%20
    Iliad%20(%CE%9B

https://liveboldandbloom.com/05/values/list-of-values

https://www.wellandgood.com/what-is-community-care/

https://goddessgift.com/goddesses/hestia/

About the Author

Irisanya Moon is a priestess, teacher, and initiate in the Reclaiming tradition. She has taught classes and camps around the world, including in the US, Canada, UK, and Australia. Irisanya writes a regular blog, *Charged by the Goddess*, for Patheos, as well as a Substack newsletter called Heart Magick, which can be found at https://irisanya.substack.com/
You can find out more about Irisanya's writing and teaching at...
www.irisanyamoon.com

You can find her blog at...
https://www.patheos.com/blogs/chargedbythegoddess

Books by Irisanya Moon...

Earth Spirit
Gaia: Saving Her, Saving Ourselves
Honoring the Wild: Reclaiming Witchcraft & Environmental Activism

Pagan Portals
Reclaiming Witchcraft
Aphrodite – Encountering the Goddess of Love & Beauty & Initiation
Iris – Goddess of the Rainbow and Messenger of the Godds
The Norns – Weavers of Fate and Magick
Artemis – Goddess of the Wild Hunt & Sovereign Heart
Circe – Goddess of Sorcery

Practically Pagan
An Alternative Guide to Health & Well-being

MOON BOOKS

PAGANISM & SHAMANISM

What is Paganism? A religion, a spirituality, an alternative belief system, nature worship? You can find support for all these definitions (and many more) in dictionaries, encyclopaedias, and text books of religion, but subscribe to any one and the truth will evade you. Above all Paganism is a creative pursuit, an encounter with reality, an exploration of meaning and an expression of the soul. Druids, Heathens, Wiccans, and others, all contribute their insights and literary riches to the Pagan tradition. Moon Books invites you to begin or to deepen your own encounter, right here, right now.

If you have enjoyed this book, why not tell other readers by posting a review on your preferred book site.

Bestsellers from Moon Books

Pagan Portals Series
The Morrigan
Meeting the Great Queens
Morgan Daimler
Ancient and enigmatic, the Morrigan reaches out to us.
On shadowed wings and in raven's call, meet the ancient Irish
goddess of war, battle, prophecy, death, sovereignty, and magic.
Paperback: 978-1-78279-833-0 ebook: 978-1-78279-834-7

The Awen Alone
Walking the Path of the Solitary Druid
Joanna van der Hoeven
An introductory guide for the solitary Druid, The Awen Alone will
accompany you as you explore, and seek out your own place
within the natural world.
Paperback: 978-1-78279-547-6 ebook: 978-1-78279-546-9

Moon Magic
Rachel Patterson
An introduction to working with the phases of the Moon,
what they are and how to live in harmony with the lunar
year and to utilise all the magical powers it provides.
Paperback: 978-1-78279-281-9 ebook: 978-1-78279-282-6

Hekate
A Devotional
Vivienne Moss
Hekate, Queen of Witches and the Shadow-Lands,
haunts the pages of this devotional bringing magic
and enchantment into your lives.
Paperback: 978-1-78535-161-7 ebook: 978-1-78535-162-4

Bestsellers from Moon Books

Keeping Her Keys
An Introduction to Hekate's Modern Witchcraft
Cyndi Brannen
Blending Hekate, witchcraft and personal development together to create a powerful new magickal perspective.
Paperback: 978-1-78904-075-3 ebook 978-1-78904-076-0

Journey to the Dark Goddess
How to Return to Your Soul
Jane Meredith
Discover the powerful secrets of the Dark Goddess and transform your depression, grief and pain into healing and integration.
Paperback: 978-1-84694-677-6 ebook: 978-1-78099-223-5

Shamanic Reiki
Expanded Ways of Working with Universal Life Force Energy
Llyn Roberts, Robert Levy
Shamanism and Reiki are each powerful ways of healing; together, their power multiplies. Shamanic Reiki introduces techniques to help healers and Reiki practitioners tap ancient healing wisdom.
Paperback: 978-1-84694-037-8 ebook: 978-1-84694-650-9

Southern Cunning
Folkloric Witchcraft in the American South
Aaron Oberon
Modern witchcraft with a Southern flair, this book is a journey through the folklore of the American South and a look at the power these stories hold for modern witches.
Paperback: 978-1-78904-196-5 ebook: 978-1-78904-197-2

Readers of ebooks can buy or view any of these bestsellers by clicking on the live link in the title. Most titles are published in paperback and as an ebook. Paperbacks are available in traditional bookshops. Both print and ebook formats are available online.

Find more titles and sign up to our readers' newsletter
http://www.johnhuntpublishing.com/paganism

For video content, author interviews and more, please subscribe to our YouTube channel.

MoonBooksPublishing

Follow us on social media for book news, promotions and more:

Facebook: Moon Books

Instagram: @MoonBooksCI

X: @MoonBooksCI

TikTok: @MoonBooksCI

Printed and bound by CPI Group (UK) Ltd, Croydon, CR0 4YY

20/01/2025

01823143-0012